So You Think You Can Coach?

10 Instructional Plays that Build Teacher Capacity!

Celeta Joyce Devine

Copyright © 2024

All Rights Reserved

Dedication

To my beloved husband, Ronald Devine,

Your unwavering support has been the cornerstone of my journey. Your encouragement, understanding, and belief in my abilities have propelled me forward every step of the way. This book stands as a testament to the strength of our partnership and the power of your steadfast love and motivation.

To my dear mother, Nedra Pruitt,

Your wisdom, guidance, and boundless love have shaped me into the person I am today. Your belief in my dreams has fueled my determination to strive for excellence. Thank you for always being my rock and my source of inspiration.

To my cherished children, Nahla Trotter and C.J. Trotter

You are my greatest blessings and my proudest accomplishments. Your passions and endless curiosity remind me of the importance of nurturing the next generation. This book is dedicated to you, with the hope that it may inspire you to chase your dreams with courage and conviction.

With heartfelt gratitude and love,

Celeta J. Devine

Acknowledgment

A special thank you to my colleagues and mentors who have provided invaluable guidance, feedback, and inspiration throughout the writing process. Your expertise and encouragement have been instrumental in shaping this book.

I am grateful to the team at Broad Horizons Consulting, LLC for their editorial guidance. I am also grateful for the designers and production staff, for their dedication and professionalism in bringing this project to life. Your passion for education and commitment to excellence are truly commendable.

Finally, I want to thank the teachers, educators, and administrators that I have the opportunity to coach and support through Diverse Learning Practices Edcuation, LLC. These are the ones who truly inspire me with their passion, dedication, and unwavering commitment to making a difference in the lives of their students. This book is dedicated to you, with the hope that it may empower you to unleash your full potential as instructional leaders and coaches.

With heartfelt gratitude,

Celeta J. Devine

Contents

Dedication iii

Acknowledgment iv

Introduction vii

Coaching Defined 1

    Tip 1- Know the Data 4

    Tip 2- Set Team Goals 29

    Tip 3- Know Your Players 56

    Tip 4: Work Plans 82

    Start with Your Personal Professional Goals as a Coach 87

        A. Professional Growth Goals 87

        B. Student Achievement Goals 87

        Consider Areas for Development 88

        Create Action Steps 89

        V. Timeline 90

        VI. Evaluation and Reflection 90

        VII. Resources Needed 90

    Tip 5: Show Don't Tell (Modeling and Guided Coaching)... 111

    Tip 6 -The Release (Observations) 127

Tip 7 – Provide Feedback and Debriefings 154

Tip 8 – Maximize Practice Time (PLC) 173

Tip 9- Resolving Conflict 206

Tip 10- Provide Motivation 224

About The Author 302

Meet the Coaches 304

Introduction

In the world of basketball, a skilled coach is like the conductor of an orchestra, orchestrating movements, strategies, and plays to lead their team to victory. Picture this: the clock is ticking down, the pressure is mounting, and in the midst of the chaos, the coach remains calm, poised, and ready to guide their players towards success. It's a scene that epitomizes the essence of coaching – the art of inspiring and empowering individuals to reach their full potential.

But what if I told you that the principles of coaching extend far beyond the basketball court? What if I told you that the same strategies used to elevate athletes can also be applied to the realm of education, where teachers are the players and students are the team?

Welcome to "So You Think You Can Coach: 10 Instructional Plays That Build Teacher Capacity." Just as a basketball coach develops plays to enhance team performance, this book provides you with ten powerful strategies to elevate your effectiveness as an instructional coach in the world of education.

Here's the scenario: you're faced with the challenge of nurturing teachers to reach their full capacity. It's a daunting task, no doubt. But fear not, because within these pages, you'll discover a playbook filled with dynamic plays designed to transform your coaching game.

Each chapter presents you with a new play – a proven method or strategy aimed at improving teacher practice and student outcomes.

But these aren't just theoretical concepts; they're hands-on techniques supported by real-world examples, actionable steps, and access to invaluable resources.

But wait, there's more. At the end of each chapter, you'll find coaching interviews that offer insights from seasoned educators, reinforcing the idea that good coaching is universal – whether on the court or in the classroom. These interviews serve as a reminder that the principles of effective coaching transcend disciplines, emphasizing the importance of building relationships, providing feedback, and fostering growth.

And let's not forget about the journal prompts sprinkled throughout the playbook. These prompts aren't just for show; they're tools for reflection – a vital component of professional growth. Because as any great educator knows, self-reflection is the cornerstone of continuous improvement.

So, grab your playbook, lace up your coaching shoes, and get ready to take your coaching game to the next level. Whether you're a seasoned coach or a rookie on the sidelines, "So You Think You Can Coach" will equip you with the strategies, insights, and inspiration you need to lead your team of teachers to victory.

Because in the game of education, as in basketball, the ultimate goal remains the same: to empower individuals, unlock potential, and achieve greatness – one play at a time.

Let the coaching begin.

So You Think You Can Coach?

Coaching Defined

At some point in most of our lives, we have all experienced a coach. When we reflect on those coaches, we realize that some stand out more than others. We differentiate them and place them on some type of scaffolded ascension or lack thereof based on criteria that may include things such as knowledge, experience, attitude, winning or losing records, motivational prowess, and much more.

A truly exceptional coach goes beyond merely imparting technical skills or achieving victories. They serve as mentors, motivators, and even life guides, shaping individuals not just as athletes but as people. Their influence extends far beyond the field or court, impacting personal growth, leadership development, and fostering a sense of camaraderie and teamwork that reverberates throughout the organization.

REFLECT- What makes a good coach?

_____

_____

_____

_____

_____

_____

_____

Celeta Joyce Devine

A coach is defined as one who instructs, prompts, and directs. What separates the good coach from the great coach is how well they complete each of those tasks. At this point, most of us are probably thinking of some sport such as tennis, football, or my personal favorite, basketball. However, let's make a quick mental shift and think about our thoughts through the lens of the beautiful world of academia.

In academia, the playing field may not be a court or a field, but rather the classroom, lecture hall, or laboratory. Here, students are the athletes, teachers the coaches, and the game? It's the pursuit of knowledge and personal growth. The stakes may seem different, but the principles remain the same.

This world of academia is as vibrant and challenging as any sports arena. It's a realm filled with eager minds, diverse talents, and the constant pursuit of excellence. But it's also a world of complexities, where bureaucracy, standardized testing, and shifting educational paradigms can sometimes cloud the path to success.

In such a dynamic environment, the role of a coach becomes paramount. Just as in sports, a great coach in academia can inspire, motivate, and guide individuals to unlock their full potential. They're not just educators; they're mentors, advocates, and champions of growth.

So, whether it's on the court or in the classroom, the essence of coaching remains unchanged. It's about nurturing talent, building character, and unleashing potential. In the beautiful world of academia, as in sports, let's embrace the spirit of coaching and rally behind the champions of tomorrow. Let's Coach!

Reflect

If you had to compose an acronym for C.O.A.C.H, what would it be? Consider your vision as an instructional coach.

C_____

O_____

A_____

C_____

H_____

Celeta Joyce Devine

Tip 1- Know the Data

And there it is, that magical word that can either make us cringe or smile. It also can have us to stick out our chest or to sink down into our desks hoping to become invisible and in need of educational resuscitation that will cause us to dust off and try again, or either quit.

DATA

What does the data say? How do we read the data? What do we need to do with the data?

Tip # 1

Know and understand the power of data. We will address this by using three simple points:

1. Read It
2. Analyze It
3. Execute It

Most educators are no strangers to getting a pile of data handed to them several times throughout the year. Some read it. Some study it. Some converse about it. The best will utilize it. Helping teachers understand data and having an appropriate plan to utilize the data can be a game changer for student outcomes.

So You Think You Can Coach?

Read It

As an instructional leader, it is crucial to emphasize the importance of thoroughly reviewing the data for each teacher before engaging in debriefings, setting goals, or any other instructional activities. Yes, all of it. Reading the data serves as the foundational step to effectively guide teachers in the right direction instructionally. There is an old saying that resonates with this notion: "To know where we are going, you have to know where we have been."

Before prioritizing efforts to "get to know" teachers on a personal level, it is essential to understand them from an instructional standpoint. Remember, the primary purpose of your role is to coach teachers, not necessarily to become their best friend. While fostering positive relationships with teachers is valuable, ensuring their professional growth and development must remain at the forefront.

By thoroughly analyzing the instructional data, you gain insights into each teacher's strengths, areas for improvement, and professional needs. This understanding enables you to tailor your coaching approach to address specific instructional challenges effectively. It also demonstrates your commitment to supporting their growth as educators.

So, before embarking on any coaching journey, take the time to delve into the instructional data. It serves as your compass, guiding you towards meaningful and impactful coaching interactions that ultimately benefit both teachers and students.

Coaching Tips

- ❖ Don't try to read all the individual data at once. Just ensure that their particular data has been read before meeting and planning with that teacher. For example, most assessment platforms will have a summary report for the school, class, individual students, etc. I would start with a class summary report that gives an overview of that teacher's performance. You might also choose something like a standard's summary report that gives you an overview of specific standards.
- ❖ If you are unfamiliar with the learning management system utilized, request training, and partner with another coach or leader who is familiar. For reference, a learning management system (LMS) is used by schools as a software platform designed to facilitate the administration, delivery, and management of educational courses, learning activities, and assessments. It provides a centralized and online space where teachers, students, and administrators can access course materials, interact with each other, track progress, and manage various aspects of the learning process, particularly assessments.
- ❖ Formulate a plan to help teachers read their data. Consider the following:
  - o Reading left to right, top to bottom, etc. Many teachers grab a report and look all around the form.

So You Think You Can Coach?

Use this order to ensure that they understand all of the aspects without missing anything and to better understand each term and level of importance. Reading in this manner helps to keep them focused.

- Meaning of unfamiliar terms- Here are a few to consider:
    - RIT- A unit of measurement used in assessments to measure student growth and performance.
    - Percentile Rank- Indicates where a student's score falls in comparison to other students nationwide or within a specific group.
    - Growth Measure- Reflects how much a student has progressed academically over a period of time, often compared to expected growth for their grade level.
    - Standard Deviation- A measure of the amount of variation or dispersion in a set of scores.
    - Learning Continuum- A framework outlining the sequence of skills and concepts students are expected to master.
    - Performance Level- Describes a student's proficiency level in relation to specific

learning standards or objectives.
- Item Analysis- Examination of individual test questions to evaluate student performance and identify areas of strengths and weakness.
- Proficiency Bands- Groupings of scores indicating different levels of mastery or achievement in a particular subject area or skill domain.
- Longitudinal Data- Data collected over time, allowing for tracking of individual student growth and trends across groups or cohorts.

❖ Healthy mindsets- Encourage teachers to think about opportunities while reading their data versus negative self-talk or penalizations. Some of these opportunities might include opportunities for growth, improvement, and possibly change.

So You Think You Can Coach?

Data Reflection Tool

Data that Makes You Say Wow	Initial Thoughts about Students	Initial Thoughts about Teaching
<ul><li>High Performing Areas</li><li>Lower Performing Areas</li><li>Unexpected Outcomes</li><li>Expected Outcomes</li></ul>	<ul><li>Consider if what the data says is in alignment with what you would expect from your students.</li><li>Consider if what the data says is not in alignment with you would expect form your students.</li></ul>	<ul><li>Consider if what the data says is in alignment with your expectations about how it was taught.</li></ul>

Questions During Initial Data Reading	

Analyze It

Now that you have guided your teachers through the process of reading the data, let's proceed to the next crucial step: data analysis. The primary purpose of analyzing data is to gain a deep understanding that enables informed decision-making and the development of actionable next steps. Ultimately, it's about charting a course forward, beginning with the end in mind.

Data analysis isn't about using data to penalize or criticize teachers. Nor is it about endlessly discussing data without purpose, or creating visually appealing data displays that serve no practical function. Instead, as aspiring coaches, our focus should be on leveraging data analysis to craft informed plans that drive meaningful change and enhance student learning outcomes.

To become effective coaches, we must master the art of synthesizing data to identify actionable next steps for both teachers and students. This involves breaking down the information into manageable components, allowing us to pinpoint precisely where teachers should focus their efforts for improvement. It's about distilling complex data into actionable insights that pave the way for tangible growth and learning.

By facilitating this process of analysis and synthesis, we empower teachers to take ownership of their professional development journey. We guide them in crafting next steps that are not only achievable but also tailored to address their specific instructional needs and the diverse learning needs of their students.

In essence, data analysis is the cornerstone of effective coaching. It equips us with the insights and understanding needed to guide teachers towards impactful action that drives student growth and learning. So, let's dive into the data, dissect it meticulously, and emerge with a clear roadmap for the journey ahead.

Coach Tips

- Provide several graphics or methods for unpacking data into smaller chunks. Create your own or research one that fits your needs. There are a ca-zillion on the market.
- Analyze the data on your own first. Find the "hot spots" both good and bad. Practice your presentation of those "hot spots" before actually meeting with teachers. Delivery is vital.
- Make a very clear and concise plan on how to coach teachers on analyzing their data. Teachers are so overwhelmed; it is the coach's job to present key information in a very simplified manner. Make it doable.

Execute It/Put it Into Play

Chances are, when we dive into the data, we'll find that student needs vary widely within a single classroom. With thirty students spread across five different levels, it can seem like an insurmountable challenge for any teacher to address each student's individual needs effectively. Many teachers default to teaching to the "middle of the road" simply because it feels like the most manageable approach, especially for novice educators who may not yet have developed more nuanced strategies.

However, this approach inevitably leaves some students underserved. Higher-achieving students may not be sufficiently challenged, while lower-achieving students can feel lost and may even become disruptive in their frustration. This is where effective coaching becomes indispensable.

As coaches, our role is to empower teachers with the tools and strategies they need to meet the diverse needs of every student in their classroom. One powerful approach is through small group instruction, particularly utilizing teacher-led stations. By implementing small group instruction, teachers can provide targeted support and enrichment to students at different levels, ensuring that each student receives the individualized attention they require.

Our mission as coaches is to guide teachers in this process, showing them how to leverage data to inform their instructional decisions and tailor their approach to meet the unique needs of each student. It's not just about teaching to the average; it's about meeting every student where they are and helping them progress from there.

Ultimately, the goal of reading and analyzing data isn't just to gather information—it's to translate that data into actionable insights that drive meaningful instruction. By supporting teachers in effectively executing these insights through targeted small group instruction, we can move beyond data analysis to genuine data execution, transforming student outcomes in the process.

Coach Tips

- Regardless of the age/grade level, coach teachers on teacher-led instruction. Lower grades are more accustomed to this, but it is imperative to incorporate it for all students at all levels. These teacher-led groups can be implemented in center rotations or during independent practice. The coach must guide teachers in committing to instruct students for short bursts of time based on their *data*.
- Be prepared to model this for your teachers to truly grasp the concept and to see quality teacher-led instruction.
- Coach teachers on planning for varied levels of data-based instruction. Plan with them.

Defining Moment

I walked into a particular school, and I can vividly recall the principal and teams going the extra mile to showcase all of their data efforts. I must admit, it was truly impressive. They had a flamboyant data rainforest adorning the hallway, meticulously coded for all to see. Each classroom boasted intricate data walls, uniformly and professionally done. Yet, the pièce de résistance of their data masterpiece was the school-wide data room, securely locked away. I had the privilege of sitting in on their data meeting, where they delved into the intricacies of student numbers. Impressive doesn't quite capture it.

However, when I visited the classrooms assigned to gauge entry points for coaching and the effectiveness of best practices, I couldn't help but notice a discrepancy. The instruction seemed lacking, to say the least, especially when compared to the magnificence of the data walls and rooms. It left me wondering: what good is all this data without a corresponding change in instruction?

The absence of utilizing data to drive instructional practices renders it pointless. Understanding student performance levels but failing to provide small group instruction based on that data is aimless. While seamless data walls adorn each room, they serve little purpose if educators only engage in whole-group instruction.

An effective instructional coach not only knows how to read the data but also guides teachers practically in utilizing it to inform crucial instructional practices such as grouping, teacher-led stations, assessments, and more. It's about translating data insights into actionable steps that directly impact student learning and growth.

So You Think You Can Coach?

Data to Instruction Form:

Standard:	Grade:

Written Standard:

Learning Targets (Based on Verbs)	Academic Vocabulary (Concepts-Nouns)	Question Stems Mastery Evidence

Celeta Joyce Devine

Lesson Ideas and Activities for Emerging Learners (Prerequisites)	Lesson Ideas and Activities for On-Level Learners (Conceptual Understanding)	Lesson Ideas and Activities for Advanced Learners (Evidence of Knowledge)

The purpose of this form is to help the coach clearly see how to differentiate a standard based lesson for low, medium and high students. Customize this document as needed for planning for differentiation with teachers.

I noticed that several pages have a horizontal on the left or right side.

So You Think You Can Coach?

Level of Data Analysis	Types of Data	Examples of Use
Classroom Level	Formative assessment, results, attendance records, student work samples	Identify areas of student need, adjust instructional strategies, track student progress.
Grade/Subject Level	Summative assessment results, standardized test scores, curriculum pacing guides	Analyze overall student performance, adjust curriculum pacing, identify trends and patterns
School/ District Level	School-wide assessment data, demographic data, teacher collaboration notes	Identify areas for school improvement, allocate resources effectively, inform professional development initiatives

The purpose of this form is to help the coach see how he/she can utilize data at different levels and to help the coaches with instructional planning.

Celeta Joyce Devine

Different Data Forms

Student Information	Name_____ Grade/Class_____	School_____ Teacher_____
Academic Performance	<ul><li>Demonstrates understanding of key concepts.</li><li>Completes assignments accurately and on time.</li><li>Actively participates in class discussions and activities.</li></ul>	**Evidence**
Classroom Behavior	<ul><li>Follows classroom rules and procedures.</li><li>Demonstrates respect towards peers and teachers.</li><li>Displays a positive attitude towards learning.</li></ul>	**Evidence**
Social and Emotional Development	<ul><li>Demonstrates good communication skills.</li></ul>	**Evidence**

So You Think You Can Coach?

	<ul><li>Works well independently as well as in group settings.</li><li>Manages emotions effectively.</li></ul>	
Areas of Improvement	<ul><li>Attention/focus in class.</li><li>Completing homework assignments.</li><li>Participation in extracurricular activities.</li></ul>	**Evidence**

Sample Benchmark

Benchmark	Date	Beginning of Year	Middle of Year	End of Year	Strengths	Opportunities for Growth

So You Think You Can Coach?

Sports Coaches Insight

Coach Coleman

Question-What is data to you?

Answer- The analysis of numbers and statistics.

Question- How do you utilize data?

Answer- Data plays a pivotal role in my decision-making process, whether it's during a game or in practice sessions. One primary way I leverage data is by utilizing it to make real-time adjustments. For instance, if the data suggests that a certain player on the opposing team is weaker in a particular aspect, I might strategically instruct one of my players to intentionally draw a foul from them. This decision isn't arbitrary; it's based on a thorough analysis of the numbers at hand. By integrating data-driven insights into my coaching strategy, I aim to maximize our team's performance and capitalize on our strengths while exploiting our opponent's weaknesses.

Question- How do you get your players to own their data?

Answer- I use film sessions. Within these sessions we pause to break down specific data. It is a part of our daily routine.

Coach Vance

Question- Talk about data.

Response- This is where I take what I have and evaluate my group one by one.

Question- Can you give me a time where data informed a decision?

Answer- One particular year, data shifted us from being a run first team to a pass first team based on the live data I was seeing with the current team.

Question- How do you get your players to own their data?

Answer- Empowering my players to take ownership of their performance data is crucial to their growth and development as athletes. One effective method I utilize is by having them complete a self-evaluation sheet. This allows them to reflect honestly on various aspects of their game, such as their position, speed, strength, and leadership skills. By giving themselves a grade ranging from A to F in these areas, they actively engage in self-assessment and take accountability for their strengths and weaknesses.

***Coach Brown** This should be moved down.*

Question- What is data?

Answer- Data is a method to measure students. Measure! Measure! Measure! Everything relates to the stats both onsite and off.

Question- How do you get your players to own their data?

Answer- I allow them to come up with their goals. I work with them to refine them. Goals in reference to stats are consistently posted and discussed. This posting may be in the form of whiteboards or charts in the practice area. I intentionally have the players stop and jot their stats in references to the goals they have set for themselves. If anyone thinks the idea of posting individualized data is cruel, they do not truly understand the essence of accountability.

Coach Trussell

Question- What is data to you?

Answer- Data is the coaching bible that we must go by.

Question- Can you just discuss data in your area of being an athletic director?

Answer- In my capacity as an athletic director, data serves as a vital tool for gaining insight into the overall landscape of our athletic programs. There's a plethora of data points I delve into, each offering valuable perspectives on different facets of our operations.

One crucial aspect is player data. This encompasses a wide array of information, including performance metrics, injury reports, academic progress, and feedback from both coaches and players. By meticulously analyzing this data, I gain a comprehensive understanding of our athletes' well-being, areas of improvement, and potential challenges they may encounter throughout the season.

Any Coach's Answers that Resonate with You	Initial Thoughts about the Coach's Response	Potential Action Steps Based on Any New Insight Discovered from the Coach's Responses

So You Think You Can Coach?

Planning for the Play

Stop and jot down some ideas for the play you read about in this sedition. How are you going to ensure this play runs well throughout the school year? Here are some key components of designing a play for you to run as an instructional leader. Think of everything you need to personally develop in this area. After you have mapped out what you need to develop, think of what you need to grow the team in this area.

1. Players, Positions, and Roles:
- *Teachers*: Central to the execution of the instructional play, teachers will serve as the frontline performers, delivering instruction and engaging students.
- *Administrators*: Providing support and resources, administrators will play a crucial role in facilitating the implementation process, ensuring alignment with school goals and objectives.
- *Instructional Coaches*: Offering guidance and expertise, instructional coaches will support teachers in honing their instructional skills and refining their practice.

2. Game Strategy:
- *Objective*: The primary aim of our instructional play is to enhance student learning outcomes by employing evidence-

based instructional practices effectively.
- *Desired Outcome*: We anticipate increased student engagement, improved mastery of learning objectives, and overall academic growth.

3. Possible Visual Representation:
- *Classrooms*: Our main stage for implementing instructional strategies, classrooms will provide the environment for active learning and application of newly acquired skills.
- *Meeting Rooms*: These spaces will facilitate collaborative planning sessions, professional development workshops, and reflective discussions aimed at refining our instructional approach.

4. Equipment:
- *Teaching Materials*: Essential resources such as textbooks, curriculum guides, technology tools, and manipulatives will support teachers in delivering effective instruction.
- *Assessment Tools*: Formative and summative assessments will help gauge student progress and inform instructional decision-making.
- *Professional Development Resources*: Books, articles, workshops, and online courses will be utilized to enhance

So You Think You Can Coach?

teachers' pedagogical knowledge and instructional practices.

5. Practice Schedule:
- *Regular Professional Learning Communities (PLCs)*: Scheduled sessions during which teachers can collaborate, practice, and refine instructional strategies in a supportive environment.
- *Professional Development Days*: Designated time for intensive training sessions focused on key components of the instructional play, allowing for deep exploration and skill development.
- *Classroom Observation and Feedback*: Opportunities for instructional leaders and peers to observe and provide constructive feedback to teachers, promoting continuous improvement and growth.

Consideration: Use the space below to map out your plan. Every component may not be needed for the play, yet feel free to add anything necessary to develop the play.

Celeta Joyce Devine

Name of Play- Data Moves

Remember to use this space to stop and jot down some ideas for the play you read about in this sedition.

So You Think You Can Coach?

Tip 2- Set Team Goals

Sean Covey coined the phrase "begin with the end in mind." I can remember being in the freshmen hallway of an awesome high school where students walked by a humongous poster banner every day that had this phrase on it. Begin with the end in mind. The idea was for the freshmen to start their high school career focusing on what they wanted at the end of their tenure as high school students. In essence, the phrase was saying to students, "This is the goal."

Goals

Setting goals serves as the foundational step towards achieving desired outcomes strategically. In the realm of education, it's imperative to teach teachers the art of setting instructional goals for students, grounded in data-driven insights. While academic proficiency and mastery are undeniably pivotal, it's equally essential to recognize the significance of personal goals for both students and educators.

Academic and Personal Goals: Aligning Aspirations

Academic goals, rooted in rigorous academic standards and performance benchmarks, form the backbone of educational endeavors. However, intertwining these with personal aspirations lends a profound sense of purpose and motivation to the pursuit of these goals. When students and educators alike align their personal aspirations with academic objectives, it ignites a powerful drive towards achievement.

Setting Team Goals: Fostering Collective Vision

Central to this discourse is the notion of setting team goals, wherein collective aspirations converge to chart a shared course of action. Before delving deeper into this concept, it's essential to acknowledge the diverse array of strategies and frameworks available to aid teams in setting and attaining their goals.

Strategies and Structures for Goal Setting: Guiding the Journey

Exploring various strategies and structures for goal setting equips teams with the tools and frameworks necessary to navigate their journey towards success effectively. From SMART goals to collaborative brainstorming sessions, the possibilities are abundant, offering teams the flexibility to tailor their approach to suit their unique needs and circumstances.

In essence, by instilling the practice of setting and pursuing goals, both academic and personal, we empower educators and students alike to embark on a purposeful journey towards excellence. This section will delve into the intricacies of setting team goals, leveraging diverse strategies and structures to foster a culture of achievement and growth within educational communities.

So You Think You Can Coach?

Here are a few:

Goal Setting Acronym	Goal Setting Methods
Six W's	1. **Who** will your goals involve? This can be professors, parents, peers, classmates, and others. 2. **What** are you trying to achieve? 3. **When** do you want to accomplish this goal? Is it an ongoing, repetitive goal? Is there a hard deadline, or is there some flexibility? 4. **Where** is this goal located? 5. **Why** is this an important goal to you? 6. **Which** resources will you need to use to accomplish this goal? Which constraints and requirements do you have in order to complete this goal?
P.A.C.T Method (formulated by Anne Laure Le Cuff)	- **Purposeful**: This step involves you looking at *what* is driving you to have this goal. - **Actionable**: In PACT, being actionable is about making progress every day without overplanning or overthinking about the future. - **Continuous**: Continuous in PACT means that you should feel free to experiment with your actions as long as you continue to make progress.

	- **Trackable**: Tracking your progress not only keeps you on track, but it allows you to reflect on how far you've come and keeps you moving forward.
S.M.A.R.T Method	→ Specific → Measurable → Attainable → Relevant → Timely

So You Think You Can Coach?

Work with your team to complete this S.M.A.R.T goal-setting exercise.

S.M.A.R.T Team Goal Worksheet

S-pecific	What do we need to do? Why do we need to accomplish this?	
M-easurable	How will we know we reached our goal? How will we measure our success?	
A-ttainable	What are some key steps we can put in place to accomplish this goal? What will we do to achieve this goal?	
R-elevant	Why is this goal important? What will achieving this goal produce?	
T-imely	When should the goal be accomplished? How often will we check in on the progress of the goal?	

Why Team Goals?

Setting clear and concise team goals is essential for any group striving for success. Without a clearly defined destination, individual members may stray onto divergent paths, leading to disparate outcomes. Here's why team goals are crucial for fostering cohesion and accountability within a group:

1. Providing Clear Direction:

- Team goals offer a beacon of clarity amidst the complexity of collaborative endeavors. By delineating a specific objective, every member understands their role and contribution towards the collective aim. This clarity ensures alignment of efforts and minimizes the risk of veering off course.

2. Aligning Individual and Team Objectives:

- Understanding the overarching goal enables individuals to discern how their specific actions contribute to the team's success. By setting clear team goals, each member gains transparency into what is expected of them independently. This alignment catalyzes personal accountability and instills a sense of ownership in achieving shared objectives.

3. Fostering Trust and Expectancy:

- Team goals serve as a catalyst for building trust among

members, fostering an environment of mutual reliance and collaboration. Each member expects their counterparts to fulfill their respective responsibilities, understanding that collective success hinges on the contribution of every individual. This shared expectation cultivates a sense of unity and purpose within the group.

4. Cultivating Personal Significance:

- Recognizing the integral role of each member in achieving team goals underscores the significance of individual contributions. It communicates to every participant that their efforts are not only valued but essential for the team's success. This realization instills a profound sense of purpose and motivation, driving individuals to give their best and strive towards collective excellence.

In essence, setting team goals is not merely about outlining objectives; it's about fostering a culture of collaboration, accountability, and trust. By establishing clear direction, aligning individual and team objectives, and nurturing a sense of expectancy, teams can navigate challenges effectively and achieve remarkable outcomes together.

Facilitating/Coaching Team Goal-Setting Sessions

In our pursuit of collective success, facilitating team goal-setting sessions is a pivotal step towards aligning our efforts and aspirations. Here's how we can conduct effective goal-setting sessions that engage participants and foster a sense of ownership:

Preparation: Before the session, ensure that participants understand the importance of goal-setting and are familiar with the chosen goal-setting framework, whether it's S.M.A.R.T Goals, PACT, or another method. Provide any necessary resources or materials to support their understanding.

Session Structure:

1. **Introduction:** Start by outlining the purpose of the goal-setting session and emphasizing the significance of collaborative goal-setting in achieving our collective objectives.

2. **Roundtable Discussion:** Encourage open dialogue among participants, allowing each member to share their perspectives, insights, and aspirations regarding team goals. As the moderator, guide the discussion to ensure that all voices are heard and that ideas are respectfully exchanged.

3. **Handout Activity:** Distribute a handout similar to the one provided below, prompting participants to reflect on their individual goals and how they align with the team's

overarching objectives. Encourage participants to jot down their thoughts and ideas for discussion.

4. **Scribe Assistance:** Designate someone to scribe the conversation, capturing key insights, decisions, and action items discussed during the session. This documentation will serve as a valuable reference for refining and finalizing team goals in subsequent sessions.

5. **Refinement:** Following the initial discussion, reconvene for a later session to refine the information related to team goals. Collaboratively review the insights gathered from the initial session and work towards crafting specific, measurable, attainable, relevant, and time-bound goals that reflect the collective vision and aspirations of the team.

Sample Handout:

Team Goal-Setting Reflection

1. **Individual Goals:** Reflect on your personal objectives and aspirations within the context of our team's mission and vision.

    - What are your individual goals for this academic year?
    - How do these goals contribute to the overall success of our team?

2. **Alignment:** Consider how your individual goals align with the broader objectives of our team.

    - In what ways do your goals support or complement the goals of our team?

    - Are there any areas of alignment that you see between your goals and the team's objectives?

3. **Collaboration:** Reflect on how collaboration with your team members can help you achieve your individual goals while advancing our collective aspirations.

    - How can collaborating with your peers enhance your ability to achieve your goals?

    - Are there any specific areas where you envision collaboration with your team members to be particularly beneficial?

4. **Next Steps:** Identify any action items or areas for further exploration that have emerged from this reflection.

    - What steps can you take to align your individual goals more closely with the team's objectives?

    - How can you contribute to the collaborative goal-setting process moving forward?

By fostering open dialogue, encouraging active participation, and providing a structured framework for reflection, we can facilitate

So You Think You Can Coach?

meaningful team goal-setting sessions that empower participants to take ownership of their collective journey towards success.

Goal Setting Reflection

Personal Goals	
Individual Professional Goals	
Grade Level Team Goals	
Department Team Goals	
Individual Goals for Parents	
Individual Goals for Parents	
School-Wide Goals	

The purpose of this form is to guide coaches in guiding their teachers in the goal-setting process. When completing the round table discussion, I would focus on the team setting goals. Encourage leaders to set goals/expectation for those contributing to teaching and learning in any capacity.

In offering feedback on the team's goal-setting process, it's crucial to emphasize alignment with the organization's overarching goals and objectives. Here's how we can ensure that the goals set forth resonate with the broader organizational vision:

1. Emphasize the Broader Picture:

- Remind the team that their goals are part of a larger framework, contributing to the organization's mission and vision. Emphasize the significance of collective alignment with organizational objectives to maximize impact and effectiveness.

2. Stress Importance of Alignment:

- Highlight the importance of ensuring that individual and team goals align seamlessly with the organization's strategic priorities. Encourage team members to reflect on how their goals contribute to advancing the organization's mission and achieving desired outcomes.

3. Provide Feedback on Clarity and Consciousness:

- Assess the clarity and consciousness of the goals presented by the team. Are the goals specific, measurable, attainable, relevant, and time-bound (SMART)? Provide constructive feedback to ensure that goals are well-defined and actionable.

- Encourage transparency and open communication to ensure that all team members have a clear understanding of the goals and their significance. Clarity promotes alignment and commitment to shared objectives.

4. Reference Point for Excellence:

- Emphasize that the goals established by the team will serve as a reference point and standard of excellence throughout the year. Encourage regular review and reflection on progress towards these goals, fostering a culture of accountability and continuous improvement.

By providing feedback that underscores the importance of alignment with organizational goals, clarity of objectives, and commitment to excellence, we can empower teams to set and pursue goals that drive meaningful impact and contribute to the overall success of the organization.

Coaching Tip

Monitor and hold participants accountable for their individual goals as well as their contribution to the team goals. Let individuals know how the monitoring and coaching conversations might look and sound like.

Coaching Tool

Goal Type			
Goal 1 for Discussion	System for Meeting Goal	Limiting factors to Meeting the Goal	Essential Needs
Goal 2 for Discussion	System for Meeting Goal	Limiting factors to Meeting the Goal	Essential Needs
Goal 3 for Discussion	System for Meeting Goal	Limiting factors to Meeting the Goal	Essential Needs

So You Think You Can Coach?

As you promote goal-setting with your team consider the following:

- → Adaptability- Goals may need to change as needs change.
- → Flexibility- Encourage willingness to adjust based on feedback.
- → Celebrate- Celebrate when goals are met with your team.
- → Perspective- View unmet goals as mere opportunities for growth that are welcomed.
- → Refinement- Goals are meant to be reviewed and refined to keep them relevant and challenging.
- → Creativity- Incorporate interactive discussions when facilitating goal-setting sessions. Keep it fun!

Feedback and Reflection- Reflection helps us to grow which should always increase student learning.

Point of Reflection

1st Corinthians 12

21 The eye cannot say to the hand, "I don't need you!" And the head cannot say to the feet, "I don't need you!" **22** On the contrary, those parts of the body that seem to be weaker are indispensable, **23** and the parts that we think are less honorable we treat with special honor. And the parts that are unpresentable are treated with special modesty, **24** while our presentable parts need no special treatment. But God has put the body together, giving greater honor to the parts that lacked it, **25** so that there should be no division in the body, but that its parts should have equal concern for each other. **26** If one part suffers, every part suffers with it; if one part is honored, every part rejoices with it. **27** Now you are the body of Christ, and each one of you is a part of it.

Your team must act and function as one body because in essence, it is. You all are one organization moving towards the same common goals.

So You Think You Can Coach?

Reflection

What insight does the above scripture give you about the importance of goal-setting and the idea of TEAM overall?

_____

_____

_____

_____

_____

_____

_____

Defining Moment

When I began my journey as a teacher, the landscape of professional development looked vastly different. The concept of SMART goals was yet to become a common practice, and discussions around setting individual or team goals were sparse. It wasn't until I transitioned into the role of an instructional coach at the building level that I recognized the transformative power of goal-setting in driving professional growth.

As an instructional coach, I made it my mission to support teachers in crafting personal and professional goals tailored to their unique aspirations, strengths, and areas for improvement. This marked a significant shift in our approach to professional development, empowering educators to take ownership of their growth journey.

However, the true turning point came when I introduced the concept of team goals to our collaborative endeavors. Recognizing the collective impact of aligned objectives, I encouraged our team to articulate goals that encompassed various aspects, from quantitative metrics to interpersonal dynamics such as communication and adherence to norms. Together, we documented these goals, setting the stage for a transformative process of accountability and shared responsibility.

The defining moment of this journey was when our team embraced these goals as guiding principles, leveraging them to inform decision-making, provide feedback, and hold one another accountable throughout the year. We engaged in meaningful discussions on how to uphold our commitments, ensuring that every member felt empowered to contribute actively towards our collective success.

As the instructional coach, my role extended beyond merely facilitating the goal-setting process. I became the guiding force, nurturing a culture of continuous improvement by encouraging regular reflection, refinement, and realignment of our team goals. By fostering a dynamic cycle of goal setting, referencing, redefining, and refining, we cultivated a sense of accountability that propelled our team towards greater heights of achievement.

In essence, the effective instructional coach serves as a steward of the goal-setting process, guiding the team in setting meaningful objectives and holding each other accountable for their attainment. Through this collaborative approach, we not only achieve our individual aspirations but also unlock the collective potential for growth and excellence.

Sports Coaches Insight

Coach Coleman

Question-How do you set goals and collaborate with players while setting those goals?

Answer- After selecting the team, there is a heavy focus on player conferences. These conferences are for both the team and the individual. I always have my personal goals set for the team, but I allow opportunities for the players to chime in on those. In addition to that, I meet with parents and all stakeholders to inform them of the goal and how they can play a role in helping us to accomplish them.

Question- What is a key element that plays a role in your personal philosophy of goal setting?

Answer- The bible says that men without vision perish. Goal-setting is the vision and the means to success.

Coach Vance

Question- How do you set goals?

Answer- One of the key things I do is to make sure that the goals set are attainable. Honestly, this may change from year to year depending on the level of players that I may have for the year.

Question- What are some examples of goals that you have set?

So You Think You Can Coach?

Answer- I am a coach that considers the whole person. So, many of my goals will consist of community service and personal goals that will often translate on the field. The vision and the mission are shared with everyone involved.

Coach Brown

Question- Talk to me about goal setting.

Response- When goal setting, you must have a baseline or starting point. This will be rooted in the data that has been gathered. This data collection will include individual data and team data.

Goal setting is in essence us figuring out how we are going to WIN. I allow student-athletes to take part in the team setting goals. I also ensure that there are individual goals set. In most cases for me that will include scholarships.

Coach Trussell

Question- How would you define goal setting?

Answer- Goal setting is a road map. It tells you where you are going and how to get there.

Question- What do you feel is the most important aspect of goal setting?

Answer- Setting both short and long-term goals is key. When short-term goals are set appropriately, they will serve as a key motivational piece for those involved. So I like to keep the goals that

I and the team have set before them frequently. I do mean EVERYONE.

Use the chart below to reflect on the previous coaches' responses and how they can resonate with you and your coaching within your building.

Any Coach's Answers that Resonate with You	Initial Thoughts about Their Response	Potential Action Steps Based on Any New Insight Discovered from their Responses
The spacing seems to be off in the above chart		

So You Think You Can Coach?

Planning for the Play

As an instructional leader, orchestrating the successful implementation of our educational "play" requires careful planning and coordination. Here's a comprehensive roadmap to ensure its smooth execution throughout the school year:

1. Players, Positions, and Roles:

- *Teachers*: Serve as the main actors, delivering instruction and facilitating learning experiences in alignment with the play's objectives.

- *Administrators*: Provide support, guidance, and resources to facilitate the implementation process, ensuring alignment with school goals and objectives.

- *Instructional Coaches*: Offer expertise and assistance in training, supporting, and coaching teachers to ensure fidelity and effectiveness in executing the play.

2. Game Strategy:

- *Objective*: The primary aim of our instructional play is to enhance student learning outcomes by implementing research-based instructional practices effectively.

- *Desired Outcome*: Increased student engagement, mastery of learning objectives, and overall academic growth.

3. Possible Visual Representation:

- *Classrooms*: Serve as the primary stage for implementing instructional strategies, providing the environment for active learning and application of newly acquired skills.
- *Meeting Rooms*: Utilized for collaborative planning sessions, professional development workshops, and reflective discussions aimed at refining our instructional approach.

4. Equipment:

- *Teaching Materials*: Textbooks, curriculum resources, technology tools, manipulatives, and other instructional materials necessary for delivering effective instruction.
- *Assessment Tools*: Formative and summative assessments to measure student progress and inform instructional decisions.
- *Professional Development Resources*: Books, articles, workshops, and online courses to enhance teachers' pedagogical knowledge and instructional practices.

5. Practice Schedule:

- *Regular Professional Learning Communities (PLCs)*: Scheduled sessions during which teachers collaborate, practice, and refine instructional strategies in a supportive environment.
- *Professional Development Days*: Designated time for

intensive training sessions focused on key components of the instructional play, allowing for deep exploration and skill development.

- *Classroom Observation and Feedback*: Opportunities for instructional leaders and peers to observe and provide constructive feedback to teachers, promoting continuous improvement and growth.

Personal Development Needs:

- *Deepening Understanding of Instructional Strategies*: Engage in ongoing professional development opportunities to enhance knowledge and expertise in evidence-based instructional practices.

- *Coaching and Mentoring Skills*: Develop effective coaching techniques to support teachers in implementing the instructional play with fidelity.

- *Data Literacy*: Strengthen skills in data analysis and interpretation to monitor the effectiveness of instructional strategies and guide decision-making.

Team Growth Needs:

- *Collaborative Planning Time*: Allocate structured time for teachers to collaborate, share best practices, and align instructional goals across grade levels and subject areas.

- *Professional Learning Communities*: Foster a culture of collaboration and continuous learning through PLCs focused on analyzing student data, refining instructional practices, and supporting each other's growth.

- *Peer Observation and Feedback*: Establish protocols for peer observation and feedback to promote a culture of shared learning and improvement among colleagues.

By addressing these key components and focusing on personal development and team growth needs, we will ensure the successful implementation and sustainability of our instructional play throughout the school year, ultimately leading to improved student outcomes and a thriving learning community.

So You Think You Can Coach?

Name of Play- Goal Setting

Stop and jot down some ideas for the play you read about in this sedition.

Tip 3- Know Your Players

Every seasoned coach understands the importance of knowing their players inside and out, don't they? Of course, they do. They know their names, their strengths, where they excel on the field, and naturally, they assess who's skilled enough to potentially make the starting lineup. After all, the ultimate aim is to clinch that championship, bask in the accolades, and hoist the trophy high.

However, I sincerely hope my assumptions are mistaken. A truly exceptional coach recognizes that success extends far beyond mere victories on the field. While it's true that in the world of sports, there may be instances where winning takes precedence, for the truly effective coach, there's a deeper understanding.

An effective coach transcends the surface-level knowledge of their team members. It's about delving into the intricacies of each individual, understanding their motivations, challenges, and aspirations. It's about recognizing the complex humanity behind the player or, in our case, the teacher.

In the realm of academics, the effective coach understands that true success isn't solely measured by test scores or accolades. It's about nurturing the holistic development of each teacher under their guidance.

So, while it's important to grasp the basics about our teachers, the mark of a truly effective coach lies in their ability to cultivate deep, meaningful relationships and support the multifaceted growth of every individual they have the privilege to coach.

The Importance of Knowing Your Teachers

Knowing your teachers is essential for developing strategic plans that maximize your coaching impact and drive desired outcomes in teaching and learning within your school.

Even if you're fortunate enough to coach in a single building, you may still find yourself responsible for coaching anywhere from 5 to 30 educators, or even more in certain cases. While it's common to prioritize a core group of teachers in more intensive coaching scenarios, a good coach aims to influence as many individuals as possible.

By intimately understanding the strengths, needs, and aspirations of each teacher, you can tailor your coaching approach to meet their specific requirements. This personalized approach allows you to develop a comprehensive plan that addresses the diverse needs of your team members while aligning with the overarching goals of your school.

In essence, knowing your teachers serves as the foundation for crafting strategic coaching plans that empower educators to thrive and ultimately enhance the teaching and learning experience for all stakeholders within your school community.

P- prioritized list of teachers based on strengths and weaknesses that align with the team goals.

L- layout of a coaching calendar that details coaching dates and times based on needs

A- actionable steps to "grow" teachers.

N- next steps which will consist of continued coaching on the same or new goal.

Prioritized lists will be determined by previous data, insight from the superior, but mostly your observations and knowledge of the teacher. This last piece is the most important. We know that there can be so many things to possibly skew data. And, we also know that one person's opinion of another can be beneficial but is not always the reality of the situation or person, but it could very well be only "their" perception. Nothing will trump your unbiased observations of your clients as you are creating your plan of prioritization. So where do we begin?

1. Make a point to view/observe all teachers in their classrooms as soon as possible.
2. Use a simple observation tool to determine 5 strengths and

possible 5 areas for growth.

3. Utilize this tool to categorize teachers in one of the following areas:

   a. Off Target   a. Today   a. High Priority

   b. On Target   b. Tomorrow   b. Medium Priority

   c. Above Target   c. Next Week   c. Low Priority

Group teachers accordingly based on the data you collected. This will help to solidify a solid coaching plan based on your knowledge of the teachers.

Check out these two coaching tools that may give you some ideas:

Teacher	Date Observed	Strengths	Coaching Opportunities
		1. 2. 3. 4. 5.	1. 2. 3. 4. 5.
		1. 2. 3. 4. 5.	1. 2. 3. 4. 5.
		1. 2. 3. 4. 5.	1. 2. 3. 4. 5.
		1. 2. 3. 4. 5.	1. 2. 3. 4. 5.

This chart is to know your participant professionally. Knowing them in this manner helps to build effective plans to have the most impact. Feel free to adapt this chart as needed.

So You Think You Can Coach?

After you have identified your teachers and their strengths and areas for growth, begin to sift through the list and determine where they fall in the three categories. Here are some things to consider as you make decisions about placement.

1. Student Engagement
2. Student Learning
3. Student Understanding
4. Productive Conversations with and Between Students
5. State Teacher Growth Rubric
6. Team/School Goals
7. Student Behavior
8. Teacher Content Knowledge
9. Teacher Questioning and Feedback
10. Classroom Management and Procedures

Yes, I am aware. This is quite a bit to think about. Just study the list. Engulf yourself in the list. Add to the list. Take away from the list. However, be sure to have a list of criteria noted in your mind as you are observing. After you have made your observations, categorize your list based on the desired outcomes of the school which I am sure is simply rooted in teaching and learning. For more clarity, ask yourself the following questions:

1. When I observed the class, which teachers had more specific concerns that would hinder student learning and success?

2. When I observed the class, which teachers had more specific traits that would enhance student learning and student success?

By systematically analyzing your observations and considering the overarching goals of teaching and learning within your school, you can categorize teachers based on their impact and identify areas for targeted support and development.

Consider the following categories of teachers.

In the field of education, teachers' development can be categorized into three distinct levels: Emergent, Proficient, and Exceptional. Let's delve into each level:

1. Emergent Teachers:

- *Definition:* Emergent teachers are typically in the early stages of their teaching career, whether they are new to the profession or transitioning into a new role. They are in the process of developing their teaching skills and gaining classroom experience.
- *Characteristics:* Emergent teachers display enthusiasm, eagerness to learn, and a willingness to try new approaches. They may be refining their classroom management

techniques and pedagogical strategies.

- *Focus:* Emergent teachers focus on building foundational skills, gaining practical experience, and seeking mentorship to support their professional growth.

2. Proficient Teachers:

- *Definition:* Proficient teachers demonstrate competence and effectiveness in their teaching practice. They have acquired the necessary skills, knowledge, and experience to facilitate learning and manage a classroom successfully.

- *Characteristics:* Proficient teachers exhibit confidence, possess strong content knowledge, and can adapt their teaching strategies to meet students' diverse needs. They maintain a supportive and engaging classroom environment.

- *Focus:* Proficient teachers aim to refine their instructional repertoire, enhance classroom management skills, and pursue ongoing professional development opportunities to improve their practice.

3. Exceptional Teachers:

- *Definition:* Exceptional teachers go above and beyond proficiency, showcasing outstanding qualities in their teaching practice. They are highly skilled, innovative, and dedicated professionals who inspire students to excel.

- *Characteristics:* Exceptional teachers are visionary leaders in education, known for their creativity, passion, and unwavering commitment to student success. They foster a culture of inquiry and academic excellence.

- *Impact:* Exceptional teachers make a profound impact on their students' academic achievement, personal growth, and overall well-being. They serve as role models and mentors, shaping students' futures through their exemplary teaching.

Understanding the distinct levels of teacher development enables educational leaders to provide targeted support and professional development opportunities tailored to teachers' evolving needs. From nurturing emergent teachers' growth to celebrating the exceptional contributions of veteran educators, fostering a culture of continuous improvement is essential for promoting excellence in teaching and learning.

So You Think You Can Coach?

Categorize your participants for effective prioritization.

Emergent	Proficient	Exceptional

The purpose of this chart is to categorize teachers based on their skill sets. Utilize this form to meet the specific needs of your school.

After you have your prioritized list, begin to chart teachers on your calendar based on individual needs. For example, you might decide that Teacher A needs to be seen three times a week while Teacher B can be seen every other week for 30 minutes or less. This will largely be determined by your number of "players" and possibly other responsibilities that you may have; therefore, no one will be able to create your coaching calendar better than you.

Actionable Steps

Actionable steps are integral to effective coaching as they provide teachers with clear guidance and direction for growth. Here's how you can incorporate actionable steps into your coaching approach:

1. **Build Relationships:** Demonstrate that you understand and value each teacher by providing personalized and meaningful feedback. Cultivate a supportive and collaborative relationship that fosters trust and rapport.

2. **Show Your Expertise:** Establish yourself as a knowledgeable and respected leader in the field of education. Offer insights and strategies that are tailored to each teacher's goals and aspirations, showcasing your expertise and credibility.

3. **Provide Customized Next Steps:** Offer actionable next

steps that align with each teacher's individual needs, goals, and aspirations. Ensure that the steps are relevant, achievable, and meaningful, empowering teachers to make tangible progress in their professional development.

By customizing your coaching calendar to meet the unique needs of each teacher and providing actionable steps for growth, you demonstrate your commitment to supporting their success and fostering a culture of continuous improvement within your school community.

Sample

Feedback	Next Steps
Students were out of their seats during instruction.	At the beginning of each class period, review your rules and procedures for getting out of their seats. As students properly adhere to the procedure, verbally praise students for following that rule. Let's keep this up for a minimum of two weeks.

Teacher Feedback Form

Feedback	Next Steps

So You Think You Can Coach?

Next Steps

Again, knowing your players will allow you to build effective plans for your coaching, an essential piece in becoming a Master Coach. This term reminds me of what one of my clients asked me.

"How do you get the teachers to do what you want?"

My response was, "I have taken out the time to KNOW them."

Because of that, asking them to shift or reconsider a practice was in most cases "no big deal" because of that "knowing relationship." They knew me, and I knew them which was a perfect recipe for TRUST which equates to shifts in practices. What are some ideas around knowing your players that will lead to developing crisp and strategic plans which will lead to growth in teacher capacity.

- → Ask them about their personal goals (over time of course).
- → Ask them about their professional goals (parallel these with the desired outcomes you set for them as well.
- → Speak! In other words, try not to ever pass by them without greeting them, and call them by their name when you do this.

- When they do something well, tell everyone. Tell them you told everyone. Create opportunities for them to share their gifts with others. This can especially be one of your "emergent" teachers. They may not be the best at teaching content, but they sure can put together a "mean" PowerPoint or MTSS folder. Shout it out!

- Try to remember their special days. Facilitate recognition for them.

- Don't be afraid to share your opportunities for growth with them, and be open to learning "from" them where appropriate. We are all professionals. I love learning from others, especially our Gen Z teachers.

- Give valuable feedback. The tone should be full of compassion and respect with several helpings of transparent and concise next steps.

- Share resources, tricks and tips with your clients that are specific to them- diversified based on needs. Even the teacher who has been teaching for 35 years will enjoy receiving tools as long as it is catered to them. This shows you "know" them.

- Be a good listener (as much as possible.) Carve out some time to just listen, especially to your high-priority teachers.

So You Think You Can Coach?

→ Allow them to have some autonomy in the coaching process. In some cases, figure out problems together. Bend in cases that will not take away from the desired outcomes of teaching and learning.

Coaching Needs Assessment Sample

Dear Teacher,

As your instructional coach, I am committed to supporting your professional growth and enhancing your teaching practice. Your input is valuable in helping me understand your needs and preferences so I can provide personalized coaching and resources that are tailored to your goals. Please take a few moments to complete this survey honestly and thoughtfully. Your responses will remain confidential.

Personal Information Name Grade/Subject Years of Teaching Experience	
Teaching Goals What are your main teaching goals for this academic year? Are there specific areas of your teaching practice that you would like to improve or develop further?	

Preferred Coaching Areas: List all that you may be interested in within the right column from highest priority to the lowest. → Classroom Management → Differentiated Instruction → Assessment and Feedback → Technology Integration → Curriculum Planning → Collaboration and Professional Learning Communities → Other (please specify)	
Professional Development What types of professional development activity or resources do you find most beneficial? (e.g., workshops, webinars, peer observations, reading materials) Are there any specific topics or areas of interest you would like to explore through professional development?	
Preferred Coaching Format How do you prefer to receive coaching support? (e.g., one-on-one meetings, group workshops, virtual sessions)	

Do you have a preferred frequency and duration for coaching sessions?	
Current Challenges or Concerns What are some challenges or concerns you are currently facing in your teaching practice? Is there anything specific you like assistance with or guidance on?	
Feedback for Improvement How can I best support you as your instructional coach? Do you have any additional comments, questions, or suggestions for improvement?	

This chart can be used as a getting to know you form for teachers. Modify the form to tailor it to the needs of your coaching.

Defining Moment

A pivotal moment for me in recognizing the significance of building relationships with players/teachers occurred when I had the opportunity to coach a group of instructional coaches. Our session aimed to refine the art of providing effective feedback and observations, a task we had recently completed. It was midway through the year, and I had guided them through key strategies for delivering impactful feedback, emphasizing the importance of questioning and providing clear next steps. Despite their adherence to these techniques and their offering of concise next steps, the session fell flat. There was something missing—a vital aspect I hadn't addressed that day, something that couldn't be covered in a single session. That missing element was the relational aspect—the understanding of our teachers.

The session felt mechanical, and the participants seemed distant and disengaged. Sure, we could mark it off our checklist for providing feedback, but what we gained was a profound lesson on the significance of truly knowing the individuals we work with. When we have a genuine connection with our teachers, the feedback we provide carries more weight and is more readily accepted. Teachers are more receptive and willing to make adjustments when they sense that we understand them and have their best interests at heart professionally.

An effective instructional coach invests time in getting to know their teachers/players so that those they work with are more receptive to feedback and suggestions. In many ways, adults aren't so different from children; they don't care how much you know until they know how much you care. Thus, building relationships with your players is paramount.

So You Think You Can Coach?

Sports Coaches Insight

Coach Coleman

Question- What does it mean to "know" your players?

Answer- This means knowing the strengths and weaknesses of your players. This includes the game and life in general. In this manner, you have a method in which to build them up.

Question- How do you know and assess the strengths and weaknesses?

Answer- It used to be that I thought that I would just know. Then I decided to do something so profound, which was to ask them. This gave me more insight inon what to focus on with the individual player and I could go from there.

Question- In what ways do you adapt your coaching style to connect with different personalities based on what you know about your athlete?

Answer- I adjusted my approach from a more my way or no way approach to becoming more of a listening coach. I realized each person has their own individual purpose that they had to have a part in achieving.

Coach Vance

Question- What are some tips that you utilize to get to know your players?

Response- One of the first things I do is have one-on-one discussions with my position coaches in order to model what to do with their players because it may be hard for me to get to all players initially. One of the first things I want them to do is have a conversation with the players that have nothing to do with football. Keep the conversation going until you feel you have made the point that you care and are concerned about their well- being.

Coach Brown

Question- Talk to me about how you get to know your players.

Answer- First off, girls can be catty. They have a lot of cliques. However, I like an activity called the Round Table. I pay attention to where players sit, etc. I want to see who sits next to who or who takes initiative to sit at the seat that represents the leadership role.

I like to ask vulnerable questions. I get to listen, and their teammates get to listen in as well. Letting players get comfortable in the beginning with being vulnerable helps in the long run.

Question- How have you had to adapt your coaching based on what you have learned about your players?

Answer- Great question. I have definitely had to adapt my style based on coaching styles that players prefer. This is information that I would have gathered at the beginning of the season. This is pretty much how I try to operate as I continue to learn them. The biggest concept to remember is that everyone is different.

Coach Trussell

<u>Question</u>- How would you advise coaches to get to know their players?

Answer- Get in front of your staff "players" as soon and as much as needed. They need to see you. I like to meet one-on-one with them as soon as possible as well. In most of my one-on-one sessions, participants stated that they wanted to have better relationships with one another. When I get in front of the staff, I ask four key questions each time.

1. What are three positive aspects of the program that we should definitely keep and possibly work well?
2. What are three things that you feel could be done differently?
3. How can I help to improve the program?
4. What is one out-of-the-box idea that you have that will improve the program?

Use the chart below to reflect on the previous coaches' responses and how they can resonate with you and your coaching within your building.

Any Coach's Answers That Resonate with You	Initial Thoughts about Their Response	Potential Action Steps Based on Any New Insight Discovered from their Responses

So You Think You Can Coach?

Planning for the Play

Stop and jot some ideas for the play you read about in this section. How are you going to ensure this play runs well throughout the school year? Here are some key components of designing a play for you to run as an instructional leader. Think of everything you need to personally develop in this area. After you have mapped out what you need to develop, think of what you need in order to grow the team in this area.

1. **Players, Positions, and Roles:**
    - Identify key teachers and administrators needed to execute the play effectively.
    - Assign roles such as facilitators, coordinators, and participants based on strengths and expertise.

2. **Game Strategy:**
    - Objective: Enhance student engagement and academic achievement through interactive learning techniques.
    - Desired Outcome: Improved student performance, increased teacher collaboration, and a positive school culture.

3. **Possible Visual Representation:**
    - Utilize classrooms, meeting rooms, and common

areas for visual representation.

- Incorporate visual aids such as posters, charts, and diagrams to illustrate the play's concepts and strategies.

4. **Equipment:**

    - Gather materials such as teaching resources, technology tools, and manipulatives required for implementation.

    - Ensure accessibility to necessary resources for both teachers and students.

5. **Practice Schedule:**

    - Allocate regular time slots for rehearsals and practice sessions.

    - Develop a structured schedule for ongoing professional development and collaboration opportunities.

    - Provide opportunities for reflection and feedback to refine the play's execution.

Consideration: Use the space below to map out your plan. Every component may not be needed for the play, yet feel free to add anything necessary to develop the play.

Name of Play- Know Your Players

Remember to stop and jot down some ideas for the play you read about in this section..

Tip 4: Work Plans

A work plan can vary in meaning across different fields, but its core premise remains the same: it's a written or thought-out guide detailing how a specific objective will be achieved. In certain contexts, a project manager takes the lead in crafting the work plan, ensuring its faithful implementation. For larger projects, their primary role might involve ensuring all stakeholders have what they need to achieve the goal, or simply keeping track of progress to ensure actionable steps stay on course.

In the realm of sports, a work plan might revolve around the obvious goal of winning the championship. Here, the head coach oversees that all assistant coaches, trainers, and nutritionists are fulfilling their roles to reach this shared objective.

In essence, an effective work plan is about reaching desired outcomes by establishing clear processes for each objective. Let's delve into this five-step plan for creating a "winning" work plan.

Step 1- Identify the Desired Outcomes.

This might seem straightforward, but often it's one of the toughest tasks for a coach. The level of difficulty often hinges on the engagement of the school district or client in the planning process. Their involvement can be both a blessing and a curse. For newcomers, having a detailed plan handed to them sounds ideal, but for those with more experience, it can feel restrictive and hinder productivity.

Let's focus on those who are newer to coaching, have minimal direction, or are navigating a new district without a clear starting point—this scenario is quite common.

To begin, determining desired outcomes requires gathering feedback from various core groups, including but not limited to:

1. School District
2. The School
3. Teachers
4. Students
5. Community

A great coach will engage with these groups to understand their goals and desired outcomes, which will then inform the prioritization of goals and the creation of a work plan tailored to their needs. What are each group's expectations? Where do these goals rank in terms of priority? What role will you play in achieving them? Utilizing a needs questionnaire for each group can serve as a helpful starting point.

Once data is collected, prioritization becomes crucial. Identifying which factors will have the greatest impact on teaching, learning, and overall student success is a key component of this process.

Step 2-Establish a Timeline

As a coach, you can identify some things that will need to take place immediately. There will be others that may not need to take place until mid or perhaps the end of the school year. Placing items in the appropriate time zone will be essential to your work plan.

Weekly Reflections and Goal-Setting

So You Think You Can Coach?

→ Introduce myself to each teacher by the second week of school.

→ Identify teacher concerns by the fourth week of school.

→ Initial observation is complete by the end of the first month of school.

→ Observe each teacher once a week.

→ Input data two days after observing a teacher.

→ Reflect on my effectiveness weekly/monthly.

Making a Calendar/Schedule

- → Your baseline observation
- → Pre-observation meeting
- → When you model the strategy
- → Debrief and planning meeting
- → Collaborative teaching hour and debriefing time.
- → Observation and feedback time.

Staying Organized with Coaching Trackers

To help keep track of where you were, who you saw, what you talked about, and what your end goal is as a team, you will want to take careful notes. One way to do so is by keeping several different types of trackers such as:

- → Teacher Goals
- → Teacher Coaching Tracker Sheet
- → Monthly Coaching Cycle Tracker Sheet
- → Weekly Coaching Communication

Step 3 Professional Development Plans

Within any effective work plan, a good coach aims to incorporate a professional development plan. It's wise to anticipate the training and development needed throughout the coaching cycle, allowing ample time for planning and preparation to achieve excellence. Here's an outline you can use to kickstart your professional development plan for the year.

Start with Your Personal Professional Goals as a Coach

A. Professional Growth Goals

- → Enhance coaching techniques and strategies.
- → Deepen understanding of effective instructional practices.
- → Develop skills for fostering collaboration among educators.
- → Improve communication and feedback skills.

B. Student Achievement Goals

- → Increase student engagement and participation.
- → Improve student learning outcomes across diverse populations.
- → Support teachers in implementing evidence-based instructional strategies.
- → Foster a positive and inclusive learning environment.

Celeta Joyce Devine

Consider Areas for Development

A. Coaching Skills

→ Conducting effective coaching conversations

→ Providing constructive feedback to teachers

→ Utilizing data to inform coaching decisions

→ Differentiating coaching approaches based on teacher needs

B. Instructional Strategies

→ Incorporating technology into instruction

→ Differentiating instruction to meet diverse student needs

→ Implementing project-based learning or inquiry-based approaches

→ Integrating social-emotional learning into instruction

C. Collaboration and Communication

→ Building relationships with teachers and administrators

→ Facilitating effective professional learning communities

→ Cultivating a culture of trust and collaboration within the school community

→ Communicating the vision and goals of instructional coaching effectively

So You Think You Can Coach?

Create Action Steps

A. Professional Learning Opportunities

→ Attend workshops or conferences on coaching best practices.

→ Participate in online courses or webinars related to instructional strategies.

→ Join professional organizations for instructional coaches.

→ Collaborate with colleagues through peer observation and feedback sessions.

B. Reading and Research

→ Read books/articles on coaching and instructional leadership.

→ Stay updated on current research and trends in education.

→ Engage in discussions with colleagues to share insights and ideas.

Always Embed Practical Application

→ Implement coaching strategies learned in professional development sessions.

→ Co-plan and co-teach with teachers to model effective instructional practices.

→ Analyze student data to identify areas for instructional

improvement.

→ Provide ongoing support and follow-up to teachers to ensure implementation success.

V. Timeline

→ Short-Term Goals: Next 3-6 months

→ Medium-Term Goals: Next 6-12 months

→ Long-Term Goals: Next 1-3 years

VI. Evaluation and Reflection

→ Reflect regularly on progress towards goals.

→ Seek feedback from teachers, administrators, and other stakeholders.

→ Adjust professional development plan as needed based on evaluation.

VII. Resources Needed

→ Access to professional development opportunities

→ Time for collaboration with teachers

→ Support from school leadership

Take a moment to reflect on some of the possible tasks, goals, and objectives to include in your daily work plan that were listed in the professional development plan for the coach. List at least three of the items that will be simple for you to achieve and three that you feel you may need professional development in to ensure success for you and your teachers.

I believe this will be an important yet easy task for me.	I foresee needing some support with this task.

Of course, ensuring your personal growth is maximized while coaching others is paramount. Always be on the lookout for opportunities to grow.

In addition to nurturing your own professional development, you're also tasked with fostering the growth of others. I've noticed that novice coaches often struggle with where to begin with coaching in general and sometimes with what specifically they should focus on coaching. It's crucial not to sit back and wait for someone else to dictate your work plan. I've seen situations where coaches are left with basic busywork tasks unrelated to coaching.

When considering what teachers need to know and learn, consider the following:

- Classroom Observations
- Building and District Goals for Growth
- Teacher Growth Rubric

Classroom observations help tailor coaching efforts. For example, Teacher A may need support with classroom management, while Teacher B may require coaching on a specific instructional strategy for a particular outcome. Observations are invaluable for refining your coaching work plan throughout the year.

Consult with your principal and district regarding their vision and goals. Based on these goals, you can fine-tune the professional development needed to achieve them. Alignment is key for effective instructional coaching. Often, you'll serve as the bridge between the district's vision, building-level supervisors, teachers, and students.

So You Think You Can Coach?

Lastly, consider the teacher growth rubric used by your school, district, or state for end-of-year evaluations. This provides another avenue for alignment. Furthermore, it motivates teachers, as every teacher strives for the highest score. This makes the professional development you offer more meaningful and purposeful. Break down the standards into mini-professional development sessions. For instance, let's consider a standard from the Mississippi Department of Education:

Provide assignments and activities that contain the following components:

- → appropriate scaffolding that effectively builds student understanding
- → ample evidence that the teacher knows each student's level and tracks each student's progress toward the Performance Level of Mastery
- → differentiation based on students' abilities and learning styles
- → student-centered learning whenever appropriate
- → relevant connections to students' prior experiences or learning
- → opportunities for students to choose challenging tasks and instructional materials

After reading the standards and criteria for the teacher expectations, I simply pull the skill sets that I can turn into a professional development session. From the first three bullets, I can pull the following topics:

1. Scaffolding
2. Data Analysis
3. Data Grouping
4. Data Trackers
5. Differentiation
6. Types of Learning Styles

So You Think You Can Coach?

Take a moment and pull out possible professional development topics from the last three bullets.

Possible Professional Development Topics	
Topic 1	
Topic 2	
Topic 3	
Topic 4	

Next Steps

Take a moment to review the teacher growth rubric used in your school or state, and apply a similar approach to develop what you believe would be effective professional development topics. Remember to also incorporate topics based on observations and administrative visions.

Next, create a professional development calendar. Begin by selecting two topics for each month, taking into consideration the time of year. For instance, classroom management strategies might be ideal for the start of the year.

Month	Professional Development Topic
July	
August	
September	

So You Think You Can Coach?

October	
November	
December	
January	
February	
March	
April	

May	

Providing adequate professional development throughout the year will definitely be a part of your overall work plan for the school year.

Step 4 Daily Work Plans and Agendas

You will also want to consider daily and weekly work plans in order to ensure efficiency and to show direct supervisors your intent and effectiveness.

Sample A Daily Instructional Coach Work Plan

Time	Task
8:00 am	Review schedule and prioritize tasks for the day
8:15 am	Respond to urgent emails and messages
8:30 am	Plan coaching sessions and prepare materials
9:00 am	Coaching session with teacher A
10:00 am	Follow-up meeting with teacher A to discuss progress and next steps
10:30 am	Analyze student data and identify trends
11:00 am	Professional development session with select staff
12:00 pm	Lunch break

1:00 pm	Observational walkthroughs in classrooms
2:00 pm	Feedback and debriefing sessions with teachers
3:00 pm	Prepare coaching reports and documentation
3:30 pm	Collaborate with administrative staff
4:00 pm	Reflect on the day's activities and plan for tomorrow
4:30 pm	Wrap-up tasks, organize workspace
5:00 pm	End of workday

Step Five- Get Teachers Invested with Coaching Menus

A coaching menu, in the context of instructional coaching or any coaching practice, is a structured set of options or services available to clients or those we coach to address their needs, goals, and challenges. It outlines the various types of coaching support, strategies, and resources that a coach can offer to his/her clients. Consider the following for a good start:

So You Think You Can Coach?

→ **One-on-One Coaching Sessions**

- What to Expect: Personalized coaching sessions tailored to individual teacher needs and goals.
- Includes
    - Collaborative goal-setting and action planning.
    - Observation and feedback on instructional practices.
    - Co-planning and co-teaching support.
    - Data analysis and reflection on student outcomes.

→ **Group Professional Learning Workshops**

- What to Expect: Interactive workshops designed to build educator capacity and foster collaboration.
- Includes:
    - Workshops on topics such as differentiated instruction, formative assessment, and classroom management.
    - Hands-on activities and reflective discussions.
    - Sharing of best practices and resources.

→ **Data Analysis and Action Planning**

- What to Expect: Support in analyzing student data to inform instructional decision-making and goal-setting.

- Includes:
  - Data disaggregation and interpretation.
  - Identification of student learning needs and trends.
  - Development of action plans based on data insights.
  - Monitoring progress and adjusting strategies as needed.

→ **Model Lessons and Demonstration Teaching**

- What to Expect: Modeling effective instructional strategies and techniques in the classroom.
- Includes:
  - Observation of coach-led lessons or demonstration teaching.
  - Debriefing sessions to discuss instructional decisions and strategies.
  - Opportunities for teachers to observe and reflect on effective practices.

→ **Resource Sharing and Professional Development Library**

- What to Expect: Access to a curated collection of resources, tools, and professional development materials.

- Includes:
  - Digital repository of articles, videos, lesson plans, and instructional guides.
  - Book studies and discussion groups on relevant educational literature.
  - Online forums for sharing ideas and collaborating with peers.

Defining Moment

In my very first year as an instructional coach, no one told me exactly what to do or what the outline of my day should look like. There was so much freedom it seemed. Because I was passionate about being the best coach, the freedom or indication of *Mrs. Devine is just free as a bird...ineffective and free from a classroom but not actually productive* was absolutely frightening. I didn't know instructional coaching, but I did know teaching. I knew that a good teacher had a great lesson plan that was rigorous, differentiated, and slotted by times?

The effective instructional coach has an effective work plan with times and dates that maximize time and influence on teachers.

Sports Coaches Insight

Coach Coleman

Question- Can you talk to me about a work plan for a day of coaching with you?

Answer- My personal IEP had to fit within the practice plan and I could work from there. I met with players in order for them to understand their role in the work plan. Having a good work plan is very similar to a lesson plan. It must be a laid plan of action. Overtime, I had to learn to be willing to receive criticism about my work plan and its effectiveness towards productivity.

Question- Explain a key detail in which a well designed plan worked?

Answer- Of course, I know the plan is good if I am productive. My productivity depends largely on the productivity of others, so when everyone knew their roles in the work, more was accomplished. Teamwork is key to success.

Question- How do you get your players to own their data?

Answer- I use film sessions. Within these sessions we pause to break down specific data. It is a part of our daily routine.

So You Think You Can Coach?

Coach Vance

Question- Talk to us about your work plan.

Response- Because I have a pretty large staff, delegation is key. I observe the implementation of the expectations that have been set. I conference when things are not done the way I feel they should be done as the head coach of the team. This helps with productivity in the work plan.

Question- With all of that delegation, how do you ensure that the work is done effectively?

Answer- Well, individual coaching comes into play. I coach my coaches every day. This ensures that the team as a whole is hitting the mark and that the work is done how I want it done which I believe at that particular time will bring the best results. Delegation is key.

Coach Brown

Question- What is a key element to having an effective work plan?

Answer- One of the key elements to an effective work plan would be to have a written plan. Written plans should be for practice and my personal days as well. When you write things out, you are more apt to hit the heavy hitters with more fidelity and consistently.

Coach Trussell

Question- How do you ensure that you have an effective work plan?

Answer- Well, one thing my dad always told me was that if you learn how to work and work hard, you will never go hungry.

Question- What does that really mean to you?

Answer- For me this means to always work hard, to always work with passion, and to always work with a certain level of organization.

Good coaches are willing to work harder than anyone else and to work longer hours when needed. Pacing is important as well as remembering within the possible longer hours, to always Take Care of Yourself as you are working to be the best you can be.

So You Think You Can Coach?

Use the chart below to reflect on the previous coaches' responses and how they resonate with you and your coaching within your building.

Any Coach's Answers That Resonatewith You	Initial Thoughts about Their Response	Potential Action Steps Based on Any New Insight Discovered from their Responses

Planning for the Play

Take a moment to brainstorm ideas for the strategy you read about in this section. How will you ensure its success throughout the school year? Here are some essential components to consider when designing this strategy as an instructional leader. Reflect on what you personally need to develop in this area, and then think about how to grow your team in this aspect:

1. **Players, Positions, and Roles:**
    - Identify the teachers or administrators required to execute the strategy effectively.
    - Define specific roles and responsibilities for each team member based on their strengths and expertise.

2. **Game Strategy:**
    - Clearly outline the objective and desired outcomes of the strategy.
    - Develop a comprehensive plan that aligns with broader educational goals and addresses specific

needs within the school community.

3. **Possible Visual Representation:**
    - Consider utilizing classrooms, meeting rooms, or other spaces for visual aids and presentations.
    - Use diagrams, charts, or slides to visually represent key aspects of the strategy and facilitate understanding among stakeholders.

4. **Equipment:**
    - Determine the materials and resources necessary for implementing the strategy.
    - Ensure accessibility to required equipment and materials for all team members.

5. **Practice Schedule:**
    - Allocate dedicated time for rehearsals and practice sessions to refine the strategy.
    - Establish a consistent schedule for ongoing training and skill development to ensure mastery of the strategy over time.

Consideration: Utilize the space below to map out your plan. While not every component may be needed for the strategy, feel free to add any necessary elements to support its development and implementation.

Celeta Joyce Devine

Name of Play- Work Plans

Stop and jot down some ideas for the play you read about in this section.

Tip 5: Show Don't Tell (Modeling and Guided Coaching)

As an English major, I vividly recall my first encounter with the concept of "showing" rather than merely "telling" in writing. It was a revelation for me and a transformative moment for my students. Understanding this concept enabled them to infuse life into their writing, allowing readers to experience and feel what the writer intended. It was about more than just conveying information; it was about painting vivid pictures with words—like the aroma of freshly baked bread or the anticipation of a volcano's eruption.

Transitioning into coaching, I soon realized that this principle applied just as much in the world of education. Whether I was coaching at a building level or consulting across the state, one thing remained consistent: many teachers harbored a disdain for consultants. Why? Because often, consultants were perceived as overpaid individuals who simply dictated what to do without demonstrating, modeling, or having the courage to try it themselves in front of students. Unfortunately, this stereotype resonated with my own experiences.

However, I distinctly remembered a seasoned coach from early in my career who came to N.R. Burger Middle School in Hattiesburg, MS. She didn't just talk theory; she showed us how to engage students in deeper thinking during a PLC session. When someone in the group challenged her to demonstrate, she eagerly accepted, stating, "I'm a coach, but always a teacher first." With limited preparation time and facing one of the most challenging classes, she delivered a magical lesson that transformed behavior and engagement, proving the power of showing and modeling.

That day, I made a commitment to be a coach who could back up my words with actions, willing to show—even with limited preparation and any type of student. This approach has been transformative in my coaching journey, particularly in fostering trust, respect, and change:

1. Trust: Teachers need to believe in the practices and concepts you advocate.

2. Respect: By getting involved directly with "their" students, you earn respect and credibility. If students respond positively to you, teachers are more likely to follow suit.

3. Change: Ultimately, the goal is to effect change in instructional practices. When teachers trust and respect you, they are more willing to embrace change and improve their teaching methods.

So You Think You Can Coach?

Let's Look at Key Considerations when Preparing to Show and Not Just Tell.

Develop a Protocol for Modeling

Having a clear and concise protocol is crucial for successful coaching outcomes when integrating coaching within the coaching cycle. Without it, there are numerous pitfalls, with one of the most significant being the risk of unmotivated teachers using the opportunity for the coach to simply "teach their class." This defeats the purpose of genuine learning. It's akin to teachers who do all the work in the classroom, sounding competent but leaving uncertainty about what the students actually learned. The consequence is particularly troubling when students underperform on standardized assessments despite the teacher's efforts.

This often happens because proper modeling, supported by appropriate protocols or gradual release methods, was not given the opportunity to take root.

Gradual Release Method in the Classroom

I Do- Modeling

We Do- Provide Feedback as We Do it Together

Y'all Do- Group Work-Feedback is Still Provided

You Do- Independent Work

Gradual Release Method in Coaching

I Do- The Coach Models

We Do- The Coach and Teacher Do it Together

Y'all Do- The Coach and the Team Do it Together (PLC)

You Do- The Teacher Showcases What Has Been Modeled for the Coach

In essence, the effective coach is still a teacher, but just a teacher of the teacher. The same rules apply with some minor adjustments. Here are some key protocols:

→ Base modeling on the teacher needs as noted by observation, teacher survey, or guidance from the school district.

→ Share modeling expectations with the participant.
  a. I will model
      i. We will discuss and adjust based on the outcome
  b. We will co-teach
      i. We will discuss and adjust based on the outcomes
  c. I will watch you teach a form of what was modeled and provide feedback

So You Think You Can Coach?

      i.   The process will resume if necessary

Check out this Tool:

Instructional Coach Pre-Modeling Form

I am so excited about modeling for you with your students. I have listed a few things below that you can expect from this experience.

What will I do?

- → Model the lesson
- → Engage students
- → Model best classroom management strategies
- → Debrief

What will you do?

- → Fill out notes/observation form as I model
- → Assist with correction of behavior if necessary
- → Create a time-line to present the same or a variation of the lesson modeled
- → Debrief

What standard would you like modeled?	
What class period will be best to model in?	
How many students will be in this class?	
Are there any particular components of the lesson sequence that you would like to see modeled (questioning, formative assessments.)?	
What will be a good time to debrief after the lesson?	
Additional comments	

So You Think You Can Coach?

1. Share your planning process with the participant.
2. Plan with teachers where appropriate.
3. Allow the teacher to have some say so in the overall process.

Instructional Coaching Planning Document Gradual Release

→ **Establish a meeting time**

→ **Clearly coordinate what resources to bring**

→ **Discuss the goal or common point of discussion**

→ **Discuss roadblocks to student learning**

→ **Brainstorm strategies to overcome roadblocks**

→ **Share strategies connected to the goal**

→ **Establish a follow-up meeting time**

Celeta Joyce Devine

Purpose/Goal	Focus Standard	Supporting Standards	Resources

Lesson Component	Procedure/Strategies
Bell-Ringer	
Anticipatory Set (How will we introduce the lesson?)	
Modeling (I Do)	

So You Think You Can Coach?

Guided Practice (We Do)	
Guided Practice (You all Do)	
Independent Practice (You Do)	
Closing	

Plan ahead to decrease the need to have extensive preparation time in order to model.

If you desire to be the coach that can always rise to the occasion of modeling, the key is preparation:

Defining Moment

It was a chilly winter's night, and the wind whipped against my skin with such ferocity that it felt like the bite of a vampire. Just kidding... but it was a typical day in a school district where I was serving three different schools.

Things had come full circle; now, I was constantly being asked to demonstrate or model. Even if it wasn't a direct request, I knew that showing was the quickest way to earn trust and credibility with my clients.

So, I decided to compile mini-lessons for the key standards across grades 6-10, covering the range of students I worked with. It was a task, but it turned out to be the best thing for my coaching. I created electronic files for each standard and grade, diligently adding and updating as needed. While I could have used handouts or existing resources, I wanted to provide authentic instruction based on my own teaching experience. This wasn't something I could find elsewhere; I had to lay the groundwork to recreate the magic I'd experienced in previous years.

I was determined to embody the idea: "I would love to model; after all, I am a teacher first. Just give me a text and 10 to 20 minutes."

An effective coach understands that authentic modeling requires preparation. You need to have your arsenal and toolbox ready to go when called upon. Be prepared!

Provide opportunities to discuss what was modeled

After you've modeled, take some time to debrief with the teacher you're coaching. Remember, the goal is to turn every opportunity into a learning experience. Despite often being seen as experts, being open to feedback on how to enhance student learning is crucial. Here are some questions to consider:

1. What aspects of the lesson worked well?
2. What parts of the lesson could have been adjusted or improved?
3. What opportunities for growth did you notice?
4. How could we have extended the lesson to challenge more advanced students?
5. What strategies could we have used to support struggling students during the lesson?

Sports Coaches Insight

Coach Coleman

<u>Question</u>- What are some key points of effective modeling?

Answer- Stay in shape so that you can model. This would be the same as being an expert in your craft. Understand that being able to model motivates players. Players do not trust the coach who can never do what is being asked of them.

There are other simpler forms of modeling as it relates to character and professionalism. If a standard is to show up on time with no cell phone, that is exactly what I do or don't do.

Coach Vance

<u>Question</u>- Talk about modeling.

Response- Firstly, model character and expectation. Dress like a coach, carry your whistle, and be on time. Another key component that has brought me much success is to allow others to give input on what needs to be modeled.

<u>Question</u>- What happens if you feel you are not physically able to model a key skill set?

Answer- I try my best to always be in a position to model as much as I can. When I am not able to, I use a video or some other form of technology. In some cases I may use another athlete who has mastered a particular skill that I am trying to enhance in another

So You Think You Can Coach?

player.

Coach Brown

Question- How do you model for your players?

Answer- One of the first things to understand is that modeling includes less talking and more of a focus on the behavior.

Question- How would you handle modeling something that you are no longer able to do or is not within your field of expertise?

Answer- In some cases, it is ok to model without the end result. In other words, I may not need to make the shot, but I can model where to place the hands and elbows and not shoot the ball. It is absolutely ok to go to the extent of what you know.

In addition, allowing my players to watch other players is key. It may take me helping them to set that up. I have some of my players to be at the level of watching professional men to model for them to the level of what is needed.

Coach Trussell

Question- What do you think of when you think of modeling?

Answer- Well for me, I model a lot through videos and other necessary resources. Sometimes modeling can take place individually and other times modeling may need to take place with other students and coaches.

Use the chart below to reflect on the previous coaches' responses and how they can resonate with you and your coaching within your building.

Any Coach's Answers that Resonate with You	Initial Thoughts about Their Response	Potential Action Steps Based on Any New Insight Discovered from their Responses

So You Think You Can Coach?

Planning for the Play

Take a moment to brainstorm ideas for the instructional strategy you read about in this section. How will you ensure its success throughout the school year? Here are some key components to consider when designing and implementing this strategy as an instructional leader. Reflect on what you personally need to develop in this area, and then consider how to grow your team in this aspect:

1. Players, Positions, and Roles- teachers or administrators needed to accomplish the play
2. Game Strategy- objective and desired outcome
3. Possible Visual Representation- classrooms, meeting rooms
4. Equipment- materials needed for implementation
5. Practice Schedule- allocation of time to rehearse and refine the play until it becomes second nature

Consideration: Use the space below to map out your plan. Every component may not be needed for the play, yet feel free to add anything necessary to develop the play.

Name of Play- Show Don't Tell

Stop and jot down some ideas for the play you read about in this section.

Tip 6 -The Release (Observations)

Before we delve too deeply, let's consider the essence of observations. The textbook defines observation as follows: "The action or process of carefully observing something or someone in order to gain information." The pivotal phrase in this definition is "to gain information." What occurs after this scrutiny of the class is what distinguishes a good coach from a truly exceptional one. Let's break the silence and reveal it.

A good coach reports what they observed. But a GREAT coach goes beyond mere reporting; they devise a plan and actively work to ensure that this plan translates into tangible outcomes. Now that we've clarified that, let's explore the art of observation in this section. We'll delve into what follows later on.

Purpose of Observations:

1. **For Feedback:**
2. **For Action Plans:**
3. **For Teacher Development:**
4. **For Assisting with Lesson Design and Standards:**

5. **For Bolstering Classroom Management:**

6. **For Intensifying Effective Questioning:**

7. **For Supporting Classroom Layout:**

8. **For Invigorating Student Engagement:**

9. **For Identifying Entry Points to Strengthen Lesson Design:**

10. **For Identifying Entry Points for Modeling or Co-Teaching:**

The purpose of observations is to step into the classroom and gather information to facilitate a dialogue with the teacher regarding the items listed above or other potential objectives. During this discussion, you and the teacher can map out the next steps based on their personal goals and any additional objectives you deem beneficial for both the teacher and the students. Furthermore, it's crucial to consider the specific goals outlined by the principal or the district.

If I had to select the most significant purpose from the aforementioned list of ten, it would undoubtedly be identifying entry points. While a good coach simply observes, a great coach actively seeks out these entry points—opportunities to initiate the coaching cycle. Here are some key areas that the coach wants to look for:

→ Lesson Design

→ Student Understanding

→ Teacher Knowledge/Delivery

→ Classroom Management

Keystones for Lesson Design

When observing for lesson design, you actually want to look at the natural ebb and flow of the classroom. How well the sequence of the lesson is, the more students will have a clear understanding of whatever the key concept is. Additionally, sequencing a lesson provides more opportunities for scaffolding, differentiation, and ensures that the teacher is organized.

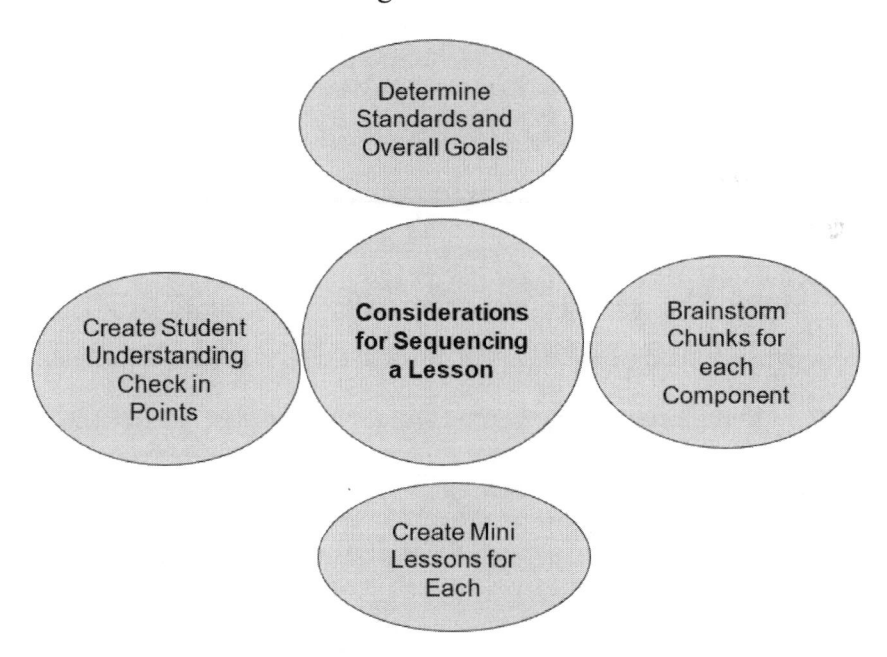

- Determine Standards and Overall Goals
- Create Student Understanding Check in Points
- **Considerations for Sequencing a Lesson**
- Brainstorm Chunks for each Component
- Create Mini Lessons for Each

When observing the teacher, look for any pieces of evidence that lend themselves to the above.

Observing to Determine Standards and Goals

When you step into a classroom, it should be immediately clear what the standard and goal for the day are. This clarity can be achieved through information posted on the board and through the teacher's verbal instructions and the activities the students are engaged in.

It's essential that the information presented to students is firmly rooted in a standard or is geared towards achieving a specific goal. If the lesson fails to do so, it's crucial to address this point in our observation feedback and debriefing session.

Many teachers may have engaging lessons that stray from the intended standard or desired student outcomes. It's important to be vigilant for this during observations. As instructional coaches, it's our responsibility to guide teachers back to the core of the standard. When we fail to do so, the gap between instructional delivery and assessment expectations widens. How often have we heard, "But I taught this"? While indeed teaching occurred, it often wasn't aligned with the standard or the goals and expectations of the assessment.

Observing for Lesson Chunking

When observing for depth of the standard and best instructional practices, there are typically three things that I notice.

1. The lesson was on target as it relates to alignment.

2. Too much of the standard was taught where there was scaffolding that needed to happen for true student understanding to take place.

3. The lesson is not rooted in the standard or inappropriate scaffolding is done.

During observations, it's important not only to listen to the teacher but also to assess whether students are truly understanding the material. Pay attention to their responses. Engage with students in a respectful manner by asking questions about their learning.

In one specific observation, the teacher focused on the development of the central idea and its effectiveness. Although students could identify the central idea, they struggled to grasp how the idea was developed. They had difficulty completing that part of the chart effectively.

In cases like this, it's essential for the teacher to step back before analyzing a writer's development and effectiveness and conduct a separate lesson on the text structures authors use to develop ideas.

During the debriefing session, we identified this misconception and made necessary adjustments.

Observing to Identify Points of Scaffolding and Creating Mini-Lessons

When the effective coach observes gaps or deficiencies in the lesson, we help that teacher break the lesson down into smaller chunks in order to close the gaps. Remember we identify the gaps through observation and focusing on student understanding or the lack thereof.

After the observation and you have noticed an area where scaffolding is needed, complete the following steps.

1. Review the standard with the teacher.
2. Identify key concepts (nouns).
3. Identify key skills (verbs).
4. Brainstorm how many lessons can be pulled out within that one standard.
5. Prioritize the mini-lessons to determine which skill sets are needed in order to complete another particular standard.
6. Work with the teacher creating a simple mini-lesson based on your findings of the standard to review.

Great observations give us direction on where to go next with the teacher.

So You Think You Can Coach?

Observing for Student Understanding through Checkpoints

When I refer to "checkpoint," I mean formative assessments. Is the teacher continuously teaching, like the energizer bunny, and ticking items off her daily teaching checklist? When observing, our main focus is on student understanding. Sometimes we coach teachers to check for student understanding throughout the lesson, not just at the end.

When teachers do this effectively, they gain insight into what students understand. When they discover misunderstandings, it provides an opportunity to correct errors before moving forward. Having checkpoints and effective formative assessments also holds students accountable. They understand that their progress will be regularly monitored throughout the learning process.

Here are some of my favorite formative assessments that also boost engagement and can be used for coaching teachers:

- → One-Minute Papers: These help assess comprehension. Students write as much as they can about a topic in one minute.
- → Gallery Walk: Students move around the room to view and interact with information or provide feedback to their peers.
- → Peer Teaching: Students explain concepts to another student or a small group while the teacher listens for understanding.

- → Jigsaw Activities: Students become experts on a specific topic or part of the material and then teach it to their peers, with the teacher listening for understanding.

- → Think-Pair-Share: Students think about a topic, pair up, and share information with a peer or the whole class.

- → Concept Maps: Students create visual representations or jot down their thoughts in a map format to show relationships between ideas.

- → Muddiest Point: Students identify the concept they found most confusing, helping the teacher identify areas that may need re-teaching.

- → Exit Tickets: Before leaving class, students answer a brief question or solve a problem related to the day's lesson. This provides insight into their understanding and allows for quick adjustments.

Observational Keystones for Lesson Design

Evidence of Lesson Design

1. Standards are Posted
2. Lesson Plans are Available
3. Standards are Aligned to State Expectations

4. Lessons are Scaffolded based on Student Data
5. Rigor should be evident

Observational Keystones for Student Understanding

Evidence of Student Understanding

1. The teacher walks around the classroom giving feedback and making adjustments
2. Peer Editing
3. Peer Feedback
4. Formative Assessments with Appropriate On-Demand Adjustments
5. Students Know and Understand Expectations
6. Collaborative Independence

Observational Keystones for Teacher Knowledge/Delivery

Evidence of Teacher Knowledge/Delivery

1. Clear and Concise Directions
2. Ability to Effectively Question Students
3. Serves as a Facilitator for Instruction
4. Use of Manipulatives or Real-World Examples
5. Leads Teacher-Led Stations Based on Data

Observational Keystones for Classroom Management

Evidence of Classroom Management

1. Organization of Classroom
2. Transitions
3. Student Compliance
4. Rules, Procedures, Consequences, and Reward Systems are Evident
5. Respectful Tones from both the Teacher and the Student

One of the key mistakes a coach can make is merely completing observations to check them off a list of tasks, without maximizing the benefits for the coaching cycle itself.

Observing teachers to identify entry points for continued coaching and learning is crucial. This method provides valuable insights into each teacher's unique strengths and areas for growth. By directly and intentionally observing classroom practices, the coach can pinpoint specific areas where the teacher excels or may need support. Effective observation allows for tailored coaching sessions that should maximize their effectiveness.

I personally recall observing a veteran teacher who was very skilled in her craft. Initially, it seemed like there was nothing for me to add as a coach, but it's my responsibility to offer insights at every level of expertise.

So You Think You Can Coach?

As I observed particular instructional strategies that were effective, I found that providing additional strategies and techniques was always appreciated. For teachers who were already excelling, offering a random strategy wasn't sufficient—they wanted strategies that would truly stretch them and align with their classroom goals. I could only do this through careful observation and studying of the teacher to provide the next steps in their career development.

A good observer looks for opportunities for the teacher that are:

Ambitious

Insightful

Relevant

The effective observation will bring air and life in the coaching situation. By using observations to take a targeted personalized approach to coaching, facilitators can maximize their impact and support teachers in reaching their full potential. It will also give the coach insight on whether to stay with a particular skill set longer or to move on to the next targeted skill.

Instructional Coaching Observation Tool for the Purpose of Coaching and Debriefing

Coaching Focus	Evidence	Opportunities
Lesson Plan Available Aligned Coherent Sequencing		
High Levels of Learning Differentiation Scaffolding Student Centered Connections		
Student Learning Feedback Formative Assessments		

So You Think You Can Coach?

Self-Assessment		
Multiple Methods Effective Questioning Connections Productive Discussion Multiple Explanations and Representations		
Management Routines Group Work Collaboration Student Behavior		
Classroom Operations Maximize Time Maximize Physical Space Classroom Transitions		

Coaching Tips:

→ Ensure that the teacher knows the purpose of the observation. This ensures that everyone is on the same page and can avoid confusion later. Of course, this will not always be the case. Some pop-in visits might be appropriate. Understand that the more we communicate about observations, the more trust and rapport we will build with our participants.

→ Occasionally consider completing a pre-observation form to meet with teachers before the observation to discuss expectations, goals, and any specific areas of focus. Teachers love the opportunity to discuss what they are doing in their classrooms. When the opportunities to discuss their practice are omitted, the participant may feel that unfair assumptions were made.

So You Think You Can Coach?

Sample Pre-Observation Form:

Teacher	
Date of Observation	
Time of Observation	
Grade/Subject	
List the Objectives and Goals of the Observation → Use of Technology → Differentiation → Small Group Instruction → Classroom Management → Questioning → Lesson Design → Assessment Practices	

→ Student Engagement → Formative Assessment → Instructional Strategies	
Instructional Goals for the Lesson	
Special Considerations for the Lesson	
Additional Comment/Notes	

Sample Post-Observation Form:

Teacher	
Date of Observation	
Time of Observation	
Grade/Subject	

So You Think You Can Coach?

Areas of Focus: (Insert Areas of Focus as Discussed in Pre-Observation Conference)	
Observed Strengths:	
Areas for Growth/Improvement:	
Evidence/Examples	
Actionable Feedback	
Reflections and Next Steps	

→

→ Consider implementing some non-intrusive observations. This is simply being mindful to not disrupt the flow of the lesson or the natural classroom environment.

→ Consider informal observations while co-teaching or parallel teaching. I have found that I can get data observations in front of the teacher while being involved simultaneously with the students.

→ Note-Taking: Take detailed, objective, and constructive notes during the observation, focusing on strengths, areas for improvement, and specific evidence to support the feedback. Remember that teachers are professionals, and we owe it to them to provide specific examples and details when asking them to modify their practices.

Defining Moment

During my first year of coaching, I struggled with the observation aspect. I wanted to be a hands-on coach, so I felt that sitting and watching was taking away from more active engagement in the classroom. However, I soon realized that teachers were asking for feedback, and I wasn't able to provide meaningful insights without collecting evidence and specific topics from effective and intentional observations.

So You Think You Can Coach?

An effective instructional coach recognizes that purposeful and deliberate observations are essential for meaningful communication and serve as entry points for coaching conversations. This shift in approach allows coaches to gather valuable insights that lead to more impactful coaching sessions and better support for teachers.

Sports Coaches Insight

Coach Coleman

<u>Question</u>- What are you looking for after you have modeled?

Answer- The release/observation serves as accountability for myself. It allows me to see two things.

1. If it doesn't look like what it needs to be, I need to model again or possibly make adjustments with players. The adjustment is only after this becomes a study point for that individual and they still do not respond to the appropriate level.
2. It allows me to know if I was successful based on if they can or cannot do it.

Coach Vance

<u>Question</u>- Talk about what you are looking for after you release players to do things on their own.

Response-

1. Understanding
2. Mastery
3. Understanding of Why

If any of these are not evident that they truly "get it," the process will begin again.

So You Think You Can Coach?

Coach Brown

<u>Question</u>- After you have modeled, what are you looking for?

Answer- I am looking to see if I need to go back to modeling at all or to determine to what extent a modeling session might occur. Within this phase, I often record players implementing the skill in order for us to have more meaningful discussions.

I am also looking for the perfection of the skill. This helps to give clear directions on the next steps as well.

In this phase, I am always looking to see if they can indeed execute the end result.

Coach Trussell

<u>Question</u>- What are some key elements of releasing your players in guided practice?

Answer- Because I am mostly working with coaches, it is important to truly *let them do it.* I look for specifics. When I participate, I am fine-tuning the details. Repetition is important, but most importantly it might be the praise that needs to take place when done correctly.

Use the chart below to reflect on the previous coaches' responses and how they can resonate with you and your coaching within your building.

Any Coach's Answers That Resonatewith You	Initial Thoughts about Their Response	Potential Action Steps Based on Any New Insight Discovered from their Responses

So You Think You Can Coach?

Planning for the Play

Stop and jot some ideas for the play you read about in this sedition. How are you going to ensure this play runs well throughout the school year? Here are some key components of designing a play for you to run as an instructional leader. Think of everything you need to personally develop in this area. After you have mapped out what you need to develop, think of what you need in order to grow the team in this area.

1. **Players, Positions, and Roles:**
    - Teachers: Actors delivering instruction and implementing strategies.
    - Administrators: Directors overseeing the overall production and providing support.
    - Instructional Coaches: Coordinators facilitating professional development and training.

2. **Game Strategy:**
    - Objective: Improve student engagement and learning outcomes.
    - Desired Outcome: Consistently high-quality instruction aligned with standards and goals.

So You Think You Can Coach?

3. **Possible Visual Representation:**

    - Classrooms: Settings for implementing instructional strategies.

    - Meeting Rooms: Spaces for planning, collaboration, and professional development.

4. **Equipment:**

    - Classroom materials: Books, technology, manipulatives.

    - Professional development resources: Workshops, training materials, curriculum guides.

5. **Practice Schedule:**

    - Weekly collaboration meetings for planning and reflecting.

    - Monthly professional development sessions focused on skill development.

    - Regular classroom observations and feedback sessions.

Personal Development Needs:

- Enhance coaching skills: Develop effective observation and feedback techniques.

- Strengthen leadership abilities: Build capacity to guide and support instructional improvement.

- Deepen content knowledge: Stay updated on curriculum standards and best practices.

Team Growth Needs:

- Professional development opportunities: Workshops on instructional strategies and classroom management.
- Collaborative planning time: Establish structured meetings for sharing ideas and refining practices.
- Continuous feedback loops: Implement systems for ongoing reflection and improvement.

By addressing these components and development areas, I aim to ensure the successful execution of the instructional play throughout the school year, fostering a culture of continuous improvement and excellence in teaching and learning.

So You Think You Can Coach?

Name of Play- Observations

Remember to stop and jot down some ideas for the play you read about in this section.

Tip 7 – Provide Feedback and Debriefings

Everyone says, "This is where the magic happens." If I had to rank the plays on a scale of 1-10, I would say that the ability to provide feedback and debriefings is #1. Picture the coach on the sidelines of an "edge of your seat" type of game. We feel the anticipation, see the lights flickering, and hear the crowd filling the stadium with applause, shouts of "D E F E N S E," and yells urging the offense to push through. Amidst this chaos, there's a still image of the coach whispering something quietly in the player's ear. This conversation, this feedback, and this brief debriefing could make the difference between winning the championship game or facing a great loss.

This interaction showcases the true skill of the coach in relaying information that brings about immediate or steady change. Providing effective feedback is indeed coaching.

Before beginning any feedback and debriefing, develop a rubric for teacher outcomes that you or your institution expects from teachers. Many states offer a "teacher growth rubric" used by administrators to complete end-of-year assessments for teachers. Starting here could make your coaching more meaningful, as aligning with the school or state's expectations can make feedback more impactful.

So You Think You Can Coach?

Essentially, it may seem like you are coaching them to achieve their best possible score.

If you choose this approach, feel free to enhance the provided teacher growth rubric based on your personal coaching goals and the teacher's own objectives. This customized approach ensures that feedback and coaching are tailored to support both professional growth and personal aspirations.

As you are considering categories to provide feedback, consider some of the following:

→ Lesson Planning and Preparation

→ Management of Time

→ Student Learning

→ Lesson Delivery

→ Classroom Management

Reflect

1. What comes to mind when you think of the idea of a self-discovery coach?

_____
_____
_____

2. What comes to mind when you think of the idea of an executive coach?

_____
_____
_____

Self Discovery Coach- One who allows input and prepares questioning in a way that the participant identifies and plays a large role in changing and refining teacher skills. It is very similar to the adage of guiding the horse to the water. This term can be somewhat synonymous with a facilitative coach.

Executive Coach- Stems from the idea of an executive who will identify the problem, create a plan of action, and strictly oversee the implementation of the plan that was created. This term can be somewhat synonymous with the idea of a more directive coach.

Reflect

What type of coach fits your natural disposition the most?
- Self-Discovery Coach
- Executive Coach

Debriefing and Feedback Questions and Statements for both the Self-Discovery and Executive Coach

Self-Discovery Coach	Executive Coach
How do you think your lesson went today?	What were some of the key issues with the lesson today?
What do you think might be the underlying reasons for this challenge?	Based on my experience, here are some strategies that could help address…
How do you envision overcoming this obstacle?	Let's establish clear objectives and action steps to tackle this problem.
Reflect on the learning or the learning gaps that took place today.	I have provided some highlights on learning for the lesson today. I have created 5 action steps for us to review that might address some of the learning gaps that I observed today.
How do you feel about the	What specific steps have you taken

progress you have made so far?	so far to address this issue
What are some alternative perspectives you could explore regarding this challenge.	Have you considered approaching the problem from a different angle?
What ideas do you have for addressing the issue, and how do you think that might work?	Based on your goals, here are some strategies I suggest you try.
What support or resources do you think you will need to achieve your goals?	What timeline do you think would be realistic to implementing these changes?
How can I best support you in moving forward with your plans?	Let's break down your goals into smaller manageable tasks. What do you think should be the first step?

So You Think You Can Coach?

Additional Coaching Tips for Effective Feedback and Debriefing

Establish a Positive Atmosphere for the Coaching Session.

One of the first things a good coach will do is warmly greet the teacher or those being coached. This sets a positive tone and helps build trust. Creating some positive banter with the teacher can also help them feel at ease and begin to establish a connection between the two of you. Think of ways you can genuinely show interest in the teacher before starting the debriefing session. Although it may seem like there's no time for this, investing in building rapport upfront saves time in the long run. Trust established during the debriefing session reduces resistance when discussing potential modifications to teaching practices.

Emphasize confidentiality during the debriefing. This is crucial. If a teacher hears that their classroom practices have been discussed negatively with others, it can damage the relationship. Keep discussions private and make the setting comfortable, whether in your office or the teacher's classroom.

End the session on a positive note. As instructional coaches, we aim to inspire change and foster hope. Even if the lesson had challenges, leave the teacher feeling optimistic about their potential for growth and mastery. This is a key aspect of being an effective instructional coach.

All in all, this is a good time to remember the *6 Golden Rules of Building Rapport:*

1. Active Listening
2. Empathy
3. Authenticity
4. Respect
5. Openness
6. Consistency

So You Think You Can Coach?

Reflect:

Take a moment to stop and jot down what each of these items will look like in your personal coaching.

Rule	Interpretation
Active Listening	
Empathy	
Authenticity	

Respect	
Openness	
Consistency	

Defining Moment

I remember leading a workshop for coaches where I asked them to identify which type of coach they were. Almost everyone prided themselves on being more directive coaches. There was a prevailing belief that the facilitative coach might be less effective than the more direct one. It sparked a great conversation!

So You Think You Can Coach?

Here's the thing though—neither approach is inherently better than the other. Most people naturally lean towards one style or the other. The key is for coaches to operate in a way that aligns with their authentic selves. The most effective coaches are those who master the art of moving fluidly between self-discovery coaching techniques and executive coaching techniques. Sometimes individuals want clear direction, while at other times, especially with adults, they need the opportunity to actively participate in their personal growth. It's about adapting to the needs of the individual and situation to achieve the best outcomes.

Sports Coaches Insight

Coach Coleman

Question-What thoughts come to mind when you think of effective feedback?

Answer- Giving critical feedback can be tricky. Everyone loves positive feedback and not much thought has to go into that. However, when we have established relationships and the expectancy of feedback, a segway to be able to "criticize" is opened.

Question- What would feedback look and sound like if I were on the field with you?

Answer- For my coaching style, you would see a lot of one on one feedback, very similar to a conference. You would hear a certain amount of level headedness and feel the presence of calmness.

Coach Vance

Question- Talk about feedback.

Response- Feedback is giving players the information they need in order to get better.

Question- What are some ways that you ensure that feedback is effective?

Answer- In some cases, I try to make sure that I speak their language. I may use some lyrics from a rap song, etc.

So You Think You Can Coach?

Question- How do you get your players to own their data?

Answer- I have players complete a self-evaluation sheet. Kids are honest. They give themselves a grade ranging from an A to an F. Some topics may include the following: position, speed, strength, and leadership. Based on what they identify, I know to work with them there because I agree with what they said, or I decide that there needs to be some mindset shifting in that area because they are inaccurate in my opinion.

Coach Brown

Question- What are your thoughts on giving feedback to your players?

Answer- One key element of the effectiveness of feedback is that it needs to be immediate. All feedback should be based on the relevant statistics.

Question- What are thoughts about tone while giving feedback? I have explained the discovery and executive styles of coaching. Which one do you fall into more naturally?

Answer- I believe that the effective coach knows how to move fluidly between the different styles. The tone very much depends on the players. I have often gained the best insight into this at the beginning of the year. Overall, I am very level-headed when giving feedback within the game. You won't hear me have very many outbursts during the times players make mistakes, and even within the small victories of the game, there will not be uncontrolled outbursts of emotion.

Coach Trussell

Question- How do you ensure effective feedback?

Answer- One of the components that is a must for those that I am giving feedback to understand the instrument that I am using. This is important and makes the process of feedback more fluid.

It is also that they understand the purpose. This may be something that we take for granted that they will know. I always like to reiterate that evaluation and feedback is for the purpose of improving quality performances and outcomes.

Question- Can you just discuss what one might see or hear during a feedback session with you?

Answer- You will definitely hear them doing a lot of talking within the sessions. I think it is important to let them talk more than you. This helps me to gauge their understanding.

Remember too, that there are all forms of feedback, and we must always be mindful of what we are relaying. For example, crossing your arms could very well be a form of feedback and could be read differently from player to player. This also brings us back to why knowing your players is so important.

So You Think You Can Coach?

Use the chart below to reflect on the previous coaches' responses and how they can resonate with you and your coaching within your building.

Any Coach's Answers That Resonate with You	Initial Thoughts about Their Response	Potential Action Steps Based on Any New Insight Discovered from their Responses

Celeta Joyce Devine

So You Think You Can Coach?

Planning for the Play

1. **Players, Positions, and Roles:**
   - Teachers: Actors delivering instructional content and implementing strategies.
   - Administrators: Directors overseeing the overall vision and providing support.
   - Instructional Coaches: Coordinators facilitating professional development and training.

2. **Game Strategy:**
   - Objective: Improve student engagement and learning outcomes.
   - Desired Outcome: Consistently high-quality instruction aligned with standards and goals.

3. **Possible Visual Representation:**
   - Classrooms: Settings for implementing instructional strategies.
   - Meeting Rooms: Spaces for planning, collaboration, and professional development.

4. **Equipment:**
   - Classroom materials: Books, technology tools, manipulatives.

- Professional development resources: Workshops, training materials, curriculum guides.

5. **Practice Schedule:**
    - Weekly collaboration meetings for planning and reflecting.
    - Monthly professional development sessions focused on skill development.
    - Regular classroom observations and feedback sessions.

Personal Development Needs:

- Enhance coaching skills: Develop effective observation and feedback techniques.
- Strengthen leadership abilities: Build capacity to guide and support instructional improvement.
- Deepen content knowledge: Stay updated on curriculum standards and best practices.

Team Growth Needs:

- Professional development opportunities: Workshops on instructional strategies and classroom management.
- Collaborative planning time: Establish structured meetings for sharing ideas and refining practices.

- Continuous feedback loops: Implement systems for ongoing reflection and improvement.

By addressing these components and development areas, I aim to ensure the successful execution of the instructional play throughout the school year. This approach fosters a collaborative environment focused on achieving meaningful outcomes for both teachers and students.

Celeta Joyce Devine

Name of Play- Feedback

Remember to stop and jot down some ideas for the play you read about in this section.

So You Think You Can Coach?

Tip 8 – Maximize Practice Time (PLC)

It's understood that much of the coaching time will occur in the classroom; however, the equivalent to the practice field in instructional coaching is within the professional learning community—the infamous PLC. This is also a great place for magic to happen. The effectiveness of the coach in bringing functionality to this dedicated time can significantly enhance coaching efforts.

One of the first things to grasp about the PLC is the distinct difference between a PLC, a meeting, and professional development. Understanding this distinction is crucial.

1. **The Meeting:** This is a venue to quickly disseminate information related to the department, school, or community. Meetings are important for communication, but it's problematic when a meeting is mistaken for a PLC.

2. **Professional Development:** This is a training session where information is shared related to a specific skill, standard, or best practice. The format is often one-sided, with a presenter and an audience. While professional development is valuable, it becomes an issue when mistaken for a PLC.

3. **The PLC:** This is where teachers collaboratively work to share knowledge, discuss data, exchange strategies, and improve teaching practices to enhance student learning outcomes.

In some cases, coaching may not be required in the area of PLCs within the building you're coaching in. Here are some indicators to help determine if or where PLC coaching might be needed.

PLC Observation Form for the Coach

Point of References	Evidence Available
Starts on Time Organized Structure is Evident	• Yes • No Evidence:
Agenda and Sign-In Sheet	• Yes • No Evidence:
Collaborative Conversation	• Yes

So You Think You Can Coach?

(Distributed Evenly)	• No Evidence:
Lesson Studies (Modeling)	• Yes • No Evidence:
Proper Feedback is Given to Teammates for Improvement	• Yes • No Evidence:
Limited Distractions	• Yes • No Evidence:
Embedded Data Discussions	• Yes • No Evidence:
Analysis of Student Work	• Yes

	- No Evidence:
Positive Atmosphere and Culture	- Yes - No Evidence:
Recommendations	
The Catalyst of all Conversation and Activities Center Around DuFour's PLC Questions: - What do we want all students to know and be able to do?	- Yes - No Evidence:

- How will we know if they learn it?
- How will we respond when some students do not learn?
- How will we extend the learning for students who are already proficient?

Instructional Coach as the Facilitator of the Facilitator

One of the key responsibilities of an instructional coach is to assist teachers in setting up the appropriate framework for a Professional Learning Community (PLC). Here's how you can guide them through the process:

1. **Tell Me:** Provide a thorough description of what an effective PLC entails. This can be done through a PowerPoint presentation, guided notes, or a detailed explanation. Outline the key components, goals, and processes of a successful PLC.

2. **Show Me:** Demonstrate what an effective PLC looks like. Show a video showcasing a well-functioning PLC in action. Organize visits to other schools or departments where the PLC framework is implemented successfully. Provide participants with handouts and materials necessary for running a PLC smoothly.

3. **Involve Me:** Encourage active involvement by giving teachers opportunities to observe and engage in effective PLCs. Arrange visits to schools or sites known for exceptional PLC practices. Sharing personal experiences of observing a perfected PLC can be powerful in illustrating the purpose and benefits of a true PLC.

Consider providing teachers with a handout outlining the benefits of observing PLCs and how it aligns with professional growth. Most schools are open to sharing their successes, so don't hesitate to reach out and request opportunities for observation.

By guiding teachers through these steps—telling them, showing them, and involving them—you can support the development and implementation of effective PLCs within your school community. This proactive approach fosters collaboration and continuous improvement among educators.

So You Think You Can Coach?

PLC Observation Form for the Teacher

Point of Reference	Description	Reflections
Goal-Setting	Are goals identified? Are there SMART goals or some variation of them?	
Planning	Are there plans constructed in order to meet those goals? What planning methods are in place?	
Collaboration and Communication	Are the members active participants? How well do they	

	communicate with one another?	
	Is the communication inclusive?	
Data Analysis	Is there evidence of data?	
	What evidence of data is present?	
	Are some of the decisions data-driven?	
Analysis of Student Work	Is there evidence on the analysis of student work?	

	Are conversations had about student work?	
	Are solutions provided for misconceptions of student understanding?	
Instructional Best Practices	What instructional strategies are present?	
	Are the teachers sharing/modeling mini-lessons?	
Professional Growth	Is there evidence that teachers collaborate outside of the PLC?	

	Is there evidence that teachers are learning to improve their practice? Are there opportunities for participants to share resources and ideas to the group?	
Overall Strengths		
Opportunities for Growth		

So You Think You Can Coach?

Signature	

Involving participants in the PLC is essential. It can be concluded that if you walk into a PLC and only one or two people doing all the talking or participation, that particular PLC is not honing in on the main purpose of a PLC. A key word is COMMUNITY. Communities engage and are active within. As the instructional coach, we must sometimes provide a blueprint of methods for engagement and involvement within the PLC.

Consider the following:

PLC Activities that Foster Involvement:

→ Article Reviews

- → Book Studies
- → Data Chats
- → Data Presentations
- → Modeling
- → Co-Teaching
- → Analyzing Student Work
- → Scoring Video Lessons for Best Practice
- → Watching Videos of the Team Members
- → Facilitating Productive Conversations

The foundation for success in involvement is allowing everyone to lead out or facilitate any of the aforementioned activities.

Key PLC Handouts for Consideration

1. Sign-in sheets to help with accountability
2. Group norms and procedures to ensure everyone is on the same page
3. Meeting agendas to provide purpose and to allow teachers to add in items that are important to them
4. Data templates that will be used throughout the year to collect and analyze data

5. Lesson study templates to provide feedback on mini-lesson provided within the PLC.
6. Meeting minutes for consistency in note taking
7. Book study templates that provide participants the opportunity to reflect on book or article studies.

Sample PLC Agenda

- → Welcome
- → Review of Previous Minutes
- → Review of Norms and Protocols
- → Review of Agenda
- → Progress Updates
- → Data Analysis and Reflection
- → Collaborative Problem Solving
- → Teacher Modeled Mini-Lesson
- → Next Steps
- → Agenda Items for Next Meeting
- → Closing

Sample Norms

- → Respect

- → Active Listening
- → Collaboration
- → Confidentiality
- → Accountability
- → Data-Based Decisions

Sample Procedures

- → Agenda Distribution
- → Facilitation
- → Time Management
- → Note-Taking
- → Follow-Up

A lesson study is simply when the educator teaches to her peers for feedback. You may have called it something different, or perhaps you called it a model lesson. I like the term lesson "study," because when it is done correctly, it becomes a means of analysis and growth in standards and teaching strategies. Here are a few practices to consider with implementation:

- → Participants to listen to provide feedback on the following during the lesson:

So You Think You Can Coach?

- ◆ Possible student misconceptions
- ◆ Clarity
- ◆ Places to extend the lesson or to scaffold

→ The teacher presenting should speak as though she is engaging with students

→ 15-20 minute lesson based on an upcoming standard from pacing or an area that the teacher desires feedback in.

Consider the following tool:

PLC Teacher Feedback Form

Teachers grow by modeling for their peers. The presenter will present as though they are presenting for students. Offer feedback using this form that will ensure that the best possible lesson is presented to students.

Teacher_____

Observer_____

Criteria	Evidence
Standard **Progression of the Standard**	
Preparedness	

So You Think You Can Coach?

Interesting/Engagement	
Clarity	
Possible Student Misconceptions	

Overall Strengths	
Overall Opportunities for Growth	

Engaging teachers in a book study within a PLC has several positive benefits. Here are a few:

- ➔ Professional Growth
- ➔ Shared Learning Experience
- ➔ Application
- ➔ Collaborative Problem Solving

So You Think You Can Coach?

Be sure to choose a book based on overall group needs or to meet a school-wide goal. Here are a few questions to use to guide teachers through the process.

PLC Book Study Guide to Strengthen Best Practices

Question	Response
How does the book's content challenge or confirm your current instructional practices?	
What specific strategies or techniques from the book do you believe could positively impact student learning in your classroom?	
How might you adapt the principles or ideas presented in the book to meet diverse needs of your students?	

What steps with you take to continually reflect on and refine your instructional practices based on feedback and ongoing learning.	
What was your favorite part of the book and why?	
What was an area of the book that you struggled with understanding as it relates to implementing it in your classroom?	
How can you incorporate the book's concepts in lesson design?	

Analyzing student work within a Professional Learning Community (PLC) is essential for fostering continuous improvement in teaching and learning practices. By collaboratively examining student work, educators gain valuable insights into the effectiveness of their instruction and the progress of their students. This process also provides opportunities for educators to reflect on their best practices.

I remember someone telling me that you can tell what the teacher has taught based on what the student produces. While this may not always be the case, it often holds true. The quality and nature of student work can reveal important information about the instructional strategies used and the depth of student understanding.

In a PLC setting, analyzing student work allows teachers to identify areas of strength and areas needing improvement. It facilitates professional discussions, the sharing of strategies, and the development of targeted interventions to better support student learning. Ultimately, this collaborative approach to analyzing student work contributes to the ongoing growth and development of educators and the improvement of outcomes for students.

Check out this guide on the thought process of analyzing student work:

Student	Assignment/Task (Describe the task and indicate the standard)	Strengths (List Strengths observed in the student's work)	Areas of Improvement (List areas where the student could improve"	Next Steps (Strategies to address areas for improvement
Student 1				
Student 2				
Student 3				
Student 4				

So You Think You Can Coach?

Defining Moment

How many times have we heard or felt that a meeting or PLC was a waste of time? "They could have just put that in an email." A defining moment for me was working with a group of teachers at the beginning of the year on effective PLCs. We covered everything: norms, feedback, data reflections, and teachers were regularly teaching to their peers.

Later in the year, a couple of those teachers approached me, begging me to ask the principal not to schedule other events during PLC time, even parent conferences should be scheduled on non-PLC days or after school, they said. They expressed, "If we miss PLC, we feel lost."

Effective instructional coaches understand the value of a PLC and know how to guide participants in implementing a finely tuned professional learning community.

Reflect

Brainstorm what procedures and norms you think would be important for PLC meetings. Keep in mind it's best to develop norms and procedures collaboratively with the team; however, it's beneficial to have some ideas in mind beforehand.

Think of norms as your "rules or expectations."

Think of procedures as your methods of operation.

Sample Norm: Arrive at 7:30 am.

Sample Procedures: Each participant will receive an email of the minutes by Tuesday. A copy is to be placed in the departmental folder.

Norms	Procedures

So You Think You Can Coach?

Sports Coaches Insight

Coach Coleman

Question- What are some key components of "practice" time?

Answer- An effective practice has to be planned for. Practice without structure typically becomes a huge waste of time. Ensuring that there is equity in time is also a key component.

It is also important to ensure equity amongst the players. All players must be productive and fully participate. In this manner, If someone can't play, I feel comfortable sending someone else in. Skills sets are necessary to develop within practice sessions.

Coach Vance

Question- How do you ensure that you have effective practice time?

Response- I have to utilize my coaches to have effective practice time. They must understand the routine and be aware of all expectations.

Delegation is of top priority.

Question- How do you handle the situation where you witness that a portion of practice may not be running as needed?

Answer- I work with the leaders. I coach my coaches every day. I may provide feedback on more effective ways for them to provide feedback. It may be a situation where I simply need to review expectations and outcomes for that particular area.

I always allow my coaches to have input. This helps with buy-in and almost always ensures that practices are effective.

Coach Brown

Question- How do you ensure that your practice time is effective?

Answer- Everyone needs to know what to expect. I have thought through it and have a written plan. I also ensure that everyone is aware of that plan. Practice always opens (warm-up) and closes (competition) in the same manner. The middle of practice may change depending on need.

I will allow players to sometimes have input because it is necessary that practice makes sense to everyone involved.

Coach Trussell

Question- What are your thoughts about having effective practice?

Answer- Some people say that practice makes perfect, but honestly I believe that perfect practice makes perfect. When it is not perfect, the exceptional coach keeps refining and making adjustments until it comes as close to perfect as they believe they can get it..

Question- How would you advise the coach to have perfect practice?

Answer- Practice should be organized. Practice should fit the audience and the needs. Practice to enhance the abilities in the room.

Everyone should be growing when practice is effective.

Use the chart below to reflect on the previous coaches' responses and how they can resonate with you and your coaching within your building.

Any Coach's Answers That Resonate with You	Initial Thoughts about Their Response	Potential Action Steps Based on Any New Insight Discovered from their Responses

So You Think You Can Coach?

Planning for the Play

Stop and jot some ideas for the play you read about in this sedition. How are you going to ensure this play runs well throughout the school year? Here are some key components of designing a play for you to run as an instructional leader. Think of everything you need to personally develop in this area. After you have mapped out what you need to develop, think of what you need in order to grow the team in this area.

1. **Players, Positions, and Roles:**
    - Teachers: Act as the main performers, delivering instruction and implementing strategies.
    - Administrators: Provide leadership and support, akin to directors overseeing the production.
    - Instructional Coaches: Serve as coordinators, facilitating professional development and training sessions.

2. **Game Strategy:**
    - Objective: Improve student engagement, understanding, and achievement.
    - Desired Outcome: Consistently high-quality teaching practices aligned with educational goals and standards.

3. **Possible Visual Representation:**

    - Classrooms: Serve as the stage for implementing instructional strategies and practices.

    - Meeting Rooms: Provide spaces for collaborative planning, reflection, and professional development sessions.

4. **Equipment:**

    - Classroom materials: Books, technology tools, manipulatives, and resources needed for effective instruction.

    - Professional development resources: Workshops, training materials, curriculum guides, and assessment tools.

5. **Practice Schedule:**

    - Weekly Collaboration Meetings: Allocate dedicated time for planning, sharing strategies, and refining instructional techniques.

    - Monthly Professional Development Sessions: Focus on skill development, reflective practice, and aligning practices with desired outcomes.

    - Regular Classroom Observations and Feedback Sessions: Provide opportunities for ongoing reflection, feedback, and refinement of teaching practices.

Personal Development Needs:

- Enhance Coaching Skills: Develop effective observation, feedback, and coaching techniques.

- Strengthen Leadership Abilities: Build capacity to guide and support instructional improvement initiatives.

- Deepen Content Knowledge: Stay updated on curriculum standards, educational trends, and research-based practices.

Team Growth Needs:

- Professional Development Opportunities: Offer workshops, seminars, and conferences focused on instructional strategies, classroom management, and educational leadership.

- Collaborative Planning Time: Establish structured meetings and collaborative sessions to share ideas, resources, and best practices.

- Continuous Feedback Loops: Implement systems for ongoing feedback, reflection, and improvement among team members.

By addressing these components and development areas, we can ensure the successful implementation and refinement of instructional practices throughout the school year. This approach fosters a collaborative and supportive environment focused on continuous improvement and positive outcomes for both educators and students.

Name of Play- Effective PLCs

Remember to stop and jot down some ideas for the play you read about in this section.

Tip 9- Resolving Conflict

Let's face it, every good team has conflict. I can remember back in my high school basketball days having some pretty heated conversations with my friends/teammates. We were like family, but on the court, we were indeed a team. The difference between a team and a family is that families tend to give passes and breaks and a lot of extra opportunities to get things right. With a team, the individuals are more apt to hold the other accountable. The mere fact of the matter is that there is no possible way for me to win if you don't win. This premise brings me to one of our many courtside fights where we had to quickly and transparently share our feelings on what we felt needed to happen, and who needed to do what. With a two-minute time constraint, the conversations often included phrases like this:

"What are you doing?"

"Get open!"

"You're not making the shot!"

"Pass me the ball!"

"Why? You're not doing anything with it."

"Everybody, get quiet- run the play to the tee."

There may have been a few extra phrases thrown in, but what was really interesting was the fact that many times the coach would just let us have at it. He didn't try to break it up if it got a "little" heated. I can remember him saying on one occasion, "There we go, get mad." He was proud of the conflict. But, we are always supposed to run from conflict or extinguish it, right?

The point to glean from this situation is that all conflict is not bad. As an effective instructional coach, it is important to first understand that and to secondly know what to do when you run into conflict on a team.

Good Conflict Vs Bad Conflict

Conflict is an inevitable aspect of human interaction, and completely avoiding it is impossible. However, not all conflicts are the same. There are healthy conflicts, which often yield positive outcomes, and unhealthy conflicts, which typically result in negative consequences. For coaches focused on fostering positive relationships in the workplace, understanding the distinction between these two types of conflicts is essential.

Healthy conflict is characterized by a willingness to engage in open and honest communication. Individuals involved in healthy conflict express their opinions without fear, yet they do so respectfully. The objective of healthy conflict is to reach a solution that satisfies all parties. In healthy conflicts, everyone involved is open to listening and considering diverse perspectives. Consequently, healthy conflict can lead to enhanced understanding, stronger relationships, and more favorable outcomes.

So how can we coach healthy conflict?

1. As the coach, realize that conflicts are inevitable, so don't be afraid of them.
2. Establish a culture where everyone understands key components of how to manifest healthy conflict when the conflict arises or before it arises.
3. Encourage participants to tell the truth; stick to the facts.
4. Encourage participants to tell the truth; stick to the facts about how they feel.
    a. Ensure the team understands the difference between invalidation and offering validation
        i. Emotional Validation is the process of learning about, understanding, and expressing acceptance of another person's emotional experience. This often leads to feelings of mutual respect and trust.
        ii. Emotional Invalidation is distinguished from emotional invalidation when a person's emotional experiences are rejected, ignored, or judged. This often leads to feelings of disrespect and division.

5. Think Win-Win- Sean Covey discusses 4 quadrants of conflict which consist of the following:

    a. WIN-WIN

    b. WIN-Lose

    c. Lose-Win

    d. Lose-Lose

When we go into conflict wanting everyone to win, it finetunes how we engage in that conflict resolution and leads to a more productive outcome.

6. Encourage participants to bring concerns to the table while also encouraging them that all concerns should focus on improving the quality of the work at hand. Personal issues not related to "the work" should follow some of the same protocols but perhaps not within a PLC, meeting, etc. and should possibly be handled by the assigned administrator.

Check out the Conflict Resolution Questionnaire for Willing Participants

Remember, the key to resolving conflict is to communicate openly and honestly, listen actively, and be willing to compromise. Good luck!

Questions	Participant One Response	Participant Two Response
1. Identify the problem: What is the issue that needs to be resolved?		
2. Define the perspectives: What are each person's perspectives on the issue? How do they see the problem?		
3. Determine shared goals: What are the shared goals that both parties have in relation to the issue?		

4. Brainstorm solutions: What are some possible solutions that can help resolve the issue? Encourage both parties to brainstorm as many solutions as possible.		
5. Evaluate solutions: Evaluate each solution-based on how well it addresses the issue and meets the shared goals.		
6. Develop an action plan: Create a plan of action for implementing the		

chosen solution. This should include specific steps, timelines, and responsibilities for each party.		
7. Choose a solution: Select the solution that both parties agree and that meets the shared goals.		
8. Follow up: Schedule a follow-up meeting to evaluate progress.		

So You Think You Can Coach?

As a coach, be like my coach who welcomed open communication about issues that were hindering the outcome of winning the "game" of education that is.

Coach Tip:

When getting ready to enter into a coaching series with teams, introduce this form or a similar form at the beginning of the coaching session or cycle to be proactive because a good team is sure to have some type of conflict. Let's welcome the conflict.

Now, on the other hand, unhealthy conflict is characterized by a lack of respect, communication, and compromise. People who engage in unhealthy conflict may resort to name-calling, yelling, or other aggressive behaviors. The goal of unhealthy conflict is often to win at all costs, regardless of how it affects others. Unhealthy conflict can lead to damaged relationships, hurt feelings, and even violence in extreme cases.

Ten Tips to Keep Conflicts Healthy

1. No Name Calling or Yelling
2. No Stone Walling
3. No Secret Methods/Silent Consequences of Trying to Get Back at the Other Person
4. Take Turns Talking
5. Listen to Understand and Not Just to Respond

6. Keep Private to Only Those it Involves

7. Remember You are on the Same Team

8. Come with an Open Mind

9. Think Win-Win

10. Keep it Focused on "The Work"

The difference between healthy and unhealthy conflict lies in the way people approach the conflict. Healthy conflict is characterized by open and honest communication, a willingness to listen to others, and a desire to find a solution that works for everyone. Unhealthy conflict, on the other hand, is marked by disrespect, aggression, and a lack of compromise. By understanding the difference between these two types of conflicts, we can help coach educators on resolving conflicts in a way that leads to positive outcomes for teaching and learning. Sometimes we must deal with the emotions, the conflicts, and the disagreements to maximize the success of teachers and students.

Reflect

Decide on your 1-2-3 step process that you will utilize to resolve conflict.

Step	Rules of Procedure
Step 1	
Step 2	
Step 3	
Step 4	
Step 5	

Defining Moment

Most individuals have little to no desire to deal with conflict. Over the years, I've learned that ignoring conflict or addressing it in small pockets almost never works. Sometimes involving the principal in a conflict discussion can be effective, but it's not always the solution. I recall being called into a conflict resolution session with two teachers due to my relationship and insight. When I entered the room, both teachers seemed visibly upset. The principal asked me to provide insight into the specifics of the conversation, but I knew this would only escalate the frustration. Instead, I focused the discussion on the work—the important tasks they both do for children, collaboratively, for the benefit of students and their parents. Emphasizing the importance of this work helped to refocus them and bring them back to center.

Effective instructional coaches understand the importance of emphasizing the passion for the work. Conflict unrelated to the work should only be addressed if it interferes with or enhances the work being done for the benefit of students. Coaches aim to ensure that participants value the work they do and keep conflicts in perspective to maintain focus and productivity.

So You Think You Can Coach?

Sports Coaches Insight

Coach Coleman

Question-What comes to mind when you think of conflict?

Answer- Conflict is simply a learning experience. Everyone has an opinion or approach to any given situation.

Question- What is your 1-2-3 step process to get through the "learning experience"?

Answer-

1. Sit both sides down together.
2. Show them both their role to the team.
3. Help them understand "in some cases" we cannot play without either of them.
4. Help them to understand how their conflict and lack of resolution can hurt the team.

Coach Vance

Question- Talk to me about conflict resolution.

Response- When there is a conflict that I need to be involved in, I get both sides together. I bring everything back to our team and individual goals. A key point for their understanding is that their conflict affects the team.

Note- I have never seen issues that are not addressed get better on their own.

Coach Brown

Question- How do you deal with conflict amongst the team?

Answer- I enjoy the round-table method. This method of sitting together is something that we establish and practice at the beginning of the season. The standards for these sessions are set ahead of time.

Question- What happens if it is a conflict with just two individuals and maybe the round-table method is not needed?

Answer- The same concept will apply. I will get those individuals together if they are unable to resolve this on their own. I will reiterate the standards of communication.

I believe that there are three types of conflict:

1. Healthy Conflict
2. Disrespectful Conflict
3. Instructional Conflict

Helping them to understand these types of conflicts is essential to me determining how involved I might need to be or if I am needed at all in the conflict resolution process.

Coach Trussell

Question- What are your thoughts on conflict and conflict resolution?

So You Think You Can Coach?

Answer- Conflicts are definitely going to happen every year.

Question- What are some of your methods for ensuring healthy conflicts?

Answer-

1. Start the conversation about conflict at the beginning of the season.

2. Set ground rules.

3. Encourage communication amongst the team through the year.

4. Always be professional.

Use the chart below to reflect on the previous coaches' responses and how they can resonate with you and your coaching within your building.

Any Coach's Answers That Resonate with You	Initial Thoughts about Their Response	Potential Action Steps Based on Any New Insight Discovered from their Responses

So You Think You Can Coach?

Planning for the Play

Stop and jot some ideas for the play you read about in this sedition. How are you going to ensure this play runs well throughout the school year? Here are some key components of designing a play for you to run as an instructional leader. Think of everything you need to personally develop in this area. After you have mapped out what you need to develop, think of what you need in order to grow the team in this area.

1. Players, Positions, and Roles- teachers or administrators needed to accomplish the play
2. Game Strategy- objective and desired outcome
3. Possible Visual Representation- classrooms, meeting rooms
4. Equipment- materials needed for implementation
5. Practice Schedule- allocation of time to rehearse and refine the play until it becomes second nature

Consideration: Use the space below to map out your plan. Every component may not be needed for the play, yet feel free to add anything necessary to develop the play.

Name of Play- Conflict Resolution

Remember to stop and jot down some ideas for the play you read about in this section.

Tip 10- Provide Motivation

MOTIVATION – One of the most common questions in the education world is how to motivate students. I used to think that the person who figured that out would become very wealthy. Over the years, my perspective has shifted. I've come to see that motivating students isn't as complex as I once believed, especially when I realized that motivation looks different for different learners. Once I grasped this, I understood that motivating students works similarly to motivating adults—it's a universal human need.

What is Motivation?

According to the first definition, motivation is the reason or reasons one has for acting or behaving in a particular way. The second definition describes motivation as the general desire or willingness of someone to do something.

Received new boot camp students daily to accommodate testing schedules.

Let's focus more on the first definition, particularly the word "reasons." As a coach, your role is to develop and create reasons for teachers to strive for their best performance. If you were to search for teacher motivation ideas online, you'd find numerous extrinsic suggestions. While these ideas are helpful and can boost motivation to a certain extent, lasting change requires intrinsic motivation. Many people mistakenly believe that intrinsic motivation is an inherent trait, but it's actually something that can be cultivated and coached.

Before delving into intrinsic motivation, let me share 50 extrinsic ideas to motivate teachers.

Teacher Motivational Tools

Gift teachers with extra time to complete tasks or create extra planning time.	Give teachers a couple of hours off work.	Ask a local business to lend a hand with tangible rewards.	Institute more casual dress days.	Listen to their concerns
Offer massage/spa gift cards.	Schedule a karaoke Day for teachers in lieu of	Have a Hawaiian style teacher	Messages to the district administrati	Mass Email Recognitio

Celeta Joyce Devine

	professional development.	barbecue.	on	n
Have a painting with a twist gatherings.	Host a cooking class for busy teachers/bring in a professional chef.	Offer health workshops for teachers.	Offer exercise programs for teachers within the school.	Host holiday parties throughout the year.
Social Media Recognition	Incorporate a teacher of the month program.	Monetary Bonuses	Stipends	Heartfelt thank-you video
Have a teacher back to school party.	Reserved parking spaces	Calendar for fun teacher events	Conference selection and attendance	Technology upgrades/subscriptions
Technology gadgets	Personalized stationery	Have a teacher year-end party.	Engraved name plate	Tickets to a local event
Membership	Provide	Dedicated	Book or e-	Audio

So You Think You Can Coach?

to a gym or fitness center	specific praise during morning or afternoon announcements	bulletin board to showcase teachers	reader with educational titles	membership
Purchase a Plant or bouquet to brighten their work space	Customized mug or tumbler	Professional photo shot to be placed on school Website	Local or school newspaper recognition	Membership to mindfulness and meditation app
Offer praise regularly	Music platform subscription	Guest expert or speaker to speak to their class	Personalized workshop or class on a topic of interest	DIY craft kit or hobby related gift
Gift Certificate to a Local Spa or Wellness Center	Subscription to an Educational Magazine or Journal	Create a Teacher Reward Program Punch Card	Team-building activity or outing with colleagues	Reduce Tasks

As mentioned earlier, one of the most important aspects of coaching teachers is motivation. A motivated teacher brings their best to the classroom and is more effective in helping students learn and grow. As an instructional coach, it's crucial to understand the importance of motivating teachers and to have strategies in place to help them stay motivated throughout the school year.

Motivating teachers can be challenging, especially when they face various demands and pressures in their personal and professional lives. However, there are several key strategies that can effectively foster intrinsic motivation among teachers. One approach is to provide regular feedback and recognition for their hard work and achievements. This can include both formal evaluations and informal praise and acknowledgment.

After conducting intentional observations, consider the following steps:

Offer Regular, Specific Feedback and Praise: Teachers often express the need for appreciation. While schools may offer treats like donuts and juice or shout-outs based on data or growth, it's essential to go beyond these gestures. After conducting observations, provide specific praise for what was observed in the classroom that supports student achievement. The more specific the feedback and praise, the more valued the teacher will feel, which can motivate them to continue excelling.

1. **Highlight Effective Practices:** Specific praise creates

excitement around teachers' practices and encourages colleagues to consider implementing new strategies. By showcasing successful practices, you inspire a culture of continuous improvement and innovation within the school community.

In summary, effective coaching involves not only offering praise but doing so in a specific and meaningful way that recognizes teachers' efforts and contributions to student success. This approach fosters a sense of purpose and accomplishment, which helps sustain intrinsic motivation throughout the school year.

Check out this chart of broad versus specific praise:

General Feedback and Praise	**Specific Feedback and Praise**
Mrs. Jones does a good job of letting her students talk in class.	Mrs. Jones has mastered Socratic Seminars which fosters student discourse. The students are excited and prepared when they are engaged in this practice. If you have been wanting some

	new ideas in this area, Mrs. Jones is an expert.
Mr. Jones has good classroom management.	Mr. Jones implemented the classroom management strategy FLEX with his students which focuses on positive redirection versus negative. Because of this, his classroom culture and climate are truly distinguished. If you have been wanting some new ideas in this area, Mr. Jones is an expert.
Mrs. Smith has great improvements in her test grades.	Mrs. Smith has incorporated what she calls a student reflection and accountability form that she uses after quizzes and some assessments. This accountability is helping her students to be more analytical

| | when testing. |
| | If you have been wanting some new ideas in the area of student academic accountability, Mrs. Smith is an expert. |

Offer Opportunities for Growth

One of the essential roles of an effective instructional coach is to instill in the teachers they work with the importance of being lifelong learners. Throughout my teaching career, I've heard the term "lifelong learner" countless times, emphasizing that it's not just a phrase but an attitude every great educator should embody. This is where I begin with the teachers I coach.

One effective way to promote lifelong learning is by identifying professional development opportunities and workshops for your teachers. This creates excitement and a sense of anticipation among educators. Not only do they get a chance to step away from the campus, but more importantly, they have the opportunity to learn from others.

Reflecting on my experience in different school districts, attending high-quality conferences and visiting other schools was transformative for me. These experiences exposed me to innovative instructional practices that enhanced my own teaching. Behind each opportunity for growth was a supportive coach advocating for these experiences, which made me feel valued and invested in.

Teachers who are provided with opportunities to learn and develop new skills are often more engaged and motivated in their work. This can involve attending conferences, workshops, receiving coaching, and mentoring support. When deciding on professional development opportunities for the teachers you coach, consider the following:

- Establish Professional Development Goals
- Address Teacher Needs Based on Observations
- Research Available Options
- Consider Timing and Logistics
- Plan Follow-Up and Implementation
- Seek Recommendations

Creating a positive and supportive school culture that values and celebrates teachers' contributions is crucial. Foster collaboration, celebrate successes, and provide ongoing support and resources to help teachers overcome challenges.

Motivating teachers is essential for fostering a positive and effective learning environment for students. By understanding the importance of motivation and implementing effective strategies to support and encourage teachers, instructional coaches play a vital role in ensuring that students receive the best education and support possible.

Reflect

Use the chart below to develop a monthly themed motivational grid for both intrinsic and extrinsic rewards.

Extrinsic- Feel free to use some Ideas from the grid in this chapter.

Intrinsic- Consider having a speaker to motivate teachers for the month. Create bulletin boards, etc. to keep the momentum going. Get everyone involved.

Month	Theme	Extrinsic Motivation Reward	Intrinsic Motivation Ideas
Example January	New Beginnings New Year New Me New Data New Start	Bundle of Classroom Supply Drawing or Give Away	Communicate Fresh Starts for Students Teachers Use Data- Consider a Motivational Staff Member, Yourself, or Outside Speaker
July			

Celeta Joyce Devine

August			
September			
October			
November			
December			
January			
February			
March			
April			
May			

So You Think You Can Coach?

Defining Moment

No cookie, intercom shout-out, or high-five is going to do the trick alone. While these gestures are positive and can contribute to motivation, they are not sufficient on their own. I once had a group of teachers who were constantly complaining about what students were not doing, and I grew tired of hearing it. I immediately launched into a motivational speech. I posed rhetorical questions about their teaching practice and dedication to education, urging them to always bring their best and to fulfill all the roles necessary to engage and guide their students effectively. I was passionate, just as I would be in the classroom with students, and I could see their lightbulbs turning on as I challenged them. My goal was to ignite a passion for their craft from within them, and it worked. Something changed in them.

Effective instructional coaches understand that true motivation comes from within for most individuals. Encouraging teachers to tap into their passion is essential for fostering long-lasting motivation. By lighting fires within teachers and inspiring them to connect with their intrinsic motivation, coaches can make a significant impact on their professional growth and effectiveness in the classroom.

Sports Coaches Insight

Coach Coleman

Question- How would you define motivation?

Answer- Motivation is bringing enthusiasm to any situation you may encounter.

Question- What are some examples of how you utilized motivational tactics?

Answer- For example, I have mixed up teams, allowing the 3rd team to take the place of some of the 1st team players. This allowed those on lower teams to feel the possibilities with hard work. This sometimes allowed 1st team players to understand the importance of not getting too comfortable.

Coach Vance

Question- What is your personal definition of motivation as it relates to coaching?

Response- It is trying to get others to accomplish their own goals.

Question- How do you go about motivating your players?

Answer- I like to remind them of their personal goals. Most of the time this does the trick. I also relate everything to the TEAM.

Question- Do you have any more tips?

Answer- Well, sometimes, players just need a simple pat on the back. I also try to speak and call everyone by name as much as possible. I do this from the star athlete to the player who possibly had not had an opportunity to get on the field the entire year.

Helping them to understand that what we do is bigger than just them. They should be motivated by the opportunity of being a part of something BIG and worthwhile.

Coach Brown

Question- How would you define motivation as it relates to your coaching?

Answer- Motivation helps someone get from point A to point B.

One way I do this is by making sure that I give players ample opportunities to see what point B looks like. This can come in the form of college tours, exposure to coaches, and overall scholarships.

Beginning with the end in mind.

I provide my players with a detailed roadmap to get to point B. I also create opportunities for frequent checkpoints to see and discuss their progress.

Coach Trussell

Question- How do you motivate players?

Answer- Always appreciate and support as much as you can. Don't be afraid to think outside of the box with those methods either.

Take the time to find out their interests and incorporate those.

Create sessions so inspiring that they don't want to miss out on which brings me to something so important and that is E-N-E-R-G-Y. Be willing to adjust your energy to get your team motivated.

Be Positive; be kind, always.

So You Think You Can Coach?

Use the chart below to reflect on the previous coaches' responses and how they resonate with you and your coaching within your building.

Any Coach's Answers That Resonate with You	Initial Thoughts about Their Response	Potential Action Steps Based on Any New Insight Discovered from their Responses

Celeta Joyce Devine

So You Think You Can Coach?

Planning for the Play

Stop and jot some ideas for the play you read about in this sedition. How are you going to ensure this play runs well throughout the school year? Here are some key components of designing a play for you to run as an instructional leader. Think of everything you need to personally develop in this area. After you have mapped out what you need to develop, think of what you need in order to grow the team in this area.

Players, Positions, and Roles- teachers or administrators needed to accomplish the play

Game Strategy- objective and desired outcome

Possible Visual Representation- classrooms, meeting rooms

Equipment- materials needed for implementation

Practice Schedule- allocation of time to rehearse and refine the play until it becomes second nature

Consideration: Use the space below to map out your plan. Every component may not be needed for the play, yet feel free to add anything necessary to develop the play.

Celeta Joyce Devine

Name of Play- Motivation

Remember to stop and jot down some ideas for the play you read about in this section.

So You Think You Can Coach?

Bonus Coaching Tip

Build TRUST

In the ever-growing world of coaching, trust serves as a cornerstone upon which growth and mastery are built.

It's a crucial element that underpins all the tips mentioned in this book, determining whether our coaching efforts thrive or fall short. Imagine trust as a bridge that spans the gap between aspiration and achievement, fixed mindsets and growth mindsets, diffidence and confidence. Exceptional coaches recognize that trust isn't just a nicety—it's a vital currency that cultivates environments conducive to exploration and evolution. Trust fosters openness, encourages vulnerability, and facilitates the exchange of insights that propel individuals toward their fullest potential.

Consider this crucial aspect of building trust:

Respecting Boundaries and Confidentiality

I recall an incident where one of my instructional leaders secretly videotaped a teacher without their consent. Afterward, the coach proceeded to show the video to everyone, not for analysis or professional development, but solely to mock the teacher's classroom management skills. Understandably, when the teacher discovered this, they were devastated, and any possibility of effective coaching was lost.

It's imperative to always respect teachers' privacy and confidentiality. Maintain professional boundaries while also remaining accessible and approachable as needed. Build trust by exemplifying the behaviors and values you expect from teachers—demonstrate integrity, fairness, and a commitment to student success. This approach will foster an environment where trust can flourish, enabling meaningful coaching relationships that benefit everyone involved.

Check out this quick list of methods of building trust from our contributing athletic coaches.

Coach Coleman
1. Be consistent both on and off the field
2. Ensure that they know their personal lives are of importance to you as well
3. Treat everyone with equality
4. Treat everyone with consistency

So You Think You Can Coach?

5. Foster a sense of comradery.

Coach Vance

1. Have limited rules
2. As the coach, do what is right
3. Know your craft
4. Hold players accountable
5. As the coach, do what you are supposed to do

Coach Brown

1. Be willing to change based on the time
2. Be willing to adjust based on the individual needs of your players
3. Allow your players to get to know you
4. Be knowledgeable
5. Know what you are talking about and how to relay that simplistically

Coach Trussell

1. Understand relationships are life and give life to any situation
2. Be kind always
3. Be consistent
4. Ensure everyone knows your expectations
5. Follow the chain of command when appropriate

Use the chart below to reflect on the previous coaches' responses and how they resonate with you and your coaching within your building.

Any Coach's Answers That Resonate with You	Initial Thoughts about Their Response	Potential Action Steps Based on Any New Insight Discovered from their Responses

So You Think You Can Coach?

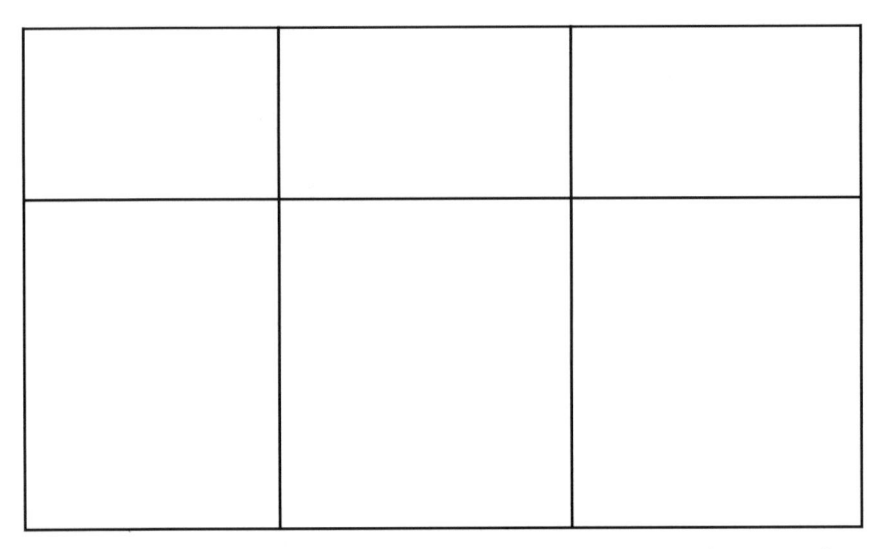

As you embark on your journey as an instructional coach, remember that at its core, this role is about revolutionizing education for the better. We must be prepared to champion what enhances teaching and learning, even if it means being direct or challenging the status quo. Knowing which strategies to employ to affect the most impactful change requires a keen understanding of effective coaching techniques.

Embrace and implement the ten foundational strategies you've learned to maximize your impact on teacher growth and systemic educational improvement. Building trust with educators is paramount, this can be done by creating an environment of open communication and collaboration. Clearly defining goals ensures that individual teacher's development aligns with broader educational objectives. By modeling excellence, providing timely feedback, and supporting reflective practices, we empower teachers to continually refine their skills.

In essence, our role is akin to calling the right play in real-time. We guide teachers in implementing effective instructional strategies that lead to achieving our ultimate goal: improving teaching and learning within our school community.

Equipping educators with resources and fostering collaboration fosters a culture of shared learning and innovation. Addressing challenges and celebrating successes are vital for maintaining momentum and morale. However, beyond these fundamental strategies lies a profound responsibility: acknowledging our capacity to drive systemic change. Coaches must advocate for policies and practices that prioritize student learning and teacher development at every level of the educational system. Through our dedication to excellent coaching, we can ignite meaningful transformation within education, shaping a brighter future for generations to come.

The Power of the Coach

In the heart of the classroom field, where dreams take flight,

Stands a coach, a leader, a source of pure light.

With wisdom and grace, they always inspire,

Igniting the spark of every aspiring desire.

Celeta Joyce Devine

The coach, the guardian of growth, and the champion of change,

In the realm of education, they rearrange.

With passion and purpose, you weave the grand scheme,

Nurturing minds like a flowing endless stream.

With every word spoken, a seed is sown,

In the fertile soil of knowledge, their players have grown.

The coach cultivates courage; the coach nurtures every soul,

In their presence, everyone feels whole.

Through challenges faced and victories won,

Their journey unfolds like the rising sun.

For the coach knows in their hearts and with unwavering trust,

Their role as a coach is a sacred must

So here's to the coaches, the unsung heroes,

Whose impact transcends the passing of zeros.

For in their hands lies the power to mold,

A future where brilliance and wisdom unfold.

Let's go get them coach!

Instructional Coach Journal Prompts

These journal prompts can serve as a starting point for self-reflection and professional growth as an instructional coach. Feel free to adapt them to suit your specific context and areas of interest.

Journal Prompt 1

Write about why you became an instructional coach.

So You Think You Can Coach?

Journal Prompt 2

Journal about any fears you have as an instructional coach. Jot down possible solutions to those fears as you discover those solutions throughout the year.

Journal Prompt 3

Journal about how you prepared or are preparing for an upcoming coaching session.

Journal Prompt 4

Reflect on a recent coaching session that you facilitated. What worked well?

Journal Prompt 5

Write about a teacher who you are looking forward to coaching and why.

So You Think You Can Coach?

Journal Prompt 6

Write about a teacher you are somewhat apprehensive about coaching and why. What can you do to get over some of those apprehensions?

Journal Prompt 7

Write out your plans for navigating through challenging teachers.

So You Think You Can Coach?

Journal Prompt 8

Journal about a recent impromptu coaching encounter.

Journal Prompt 9

Journal about a successful coaching experience where you witnessed noticeable improvement in a teacher or student learning. What factors do you attribute to the success of this coaching relationship?

So You Think You Can Coach?

Journal Prompt 10

What is one coaching strategy that you use that you will continue to replicate and refine? Why?

Journal Prompt 11

What are your strengths as a coach?

So You Think You Can Coach?

Journal Prompt 12

What are some of your personal areas of growth as a coach? Write a plan on how you will attack these areas for success.

Journal Prompt 13

Reflect on a recent coaching session. What are some things that did not work so well? Discuss some points of improvement.

So You Think You Can Coach?

Journal Prompt 14

Reflect on your communication and interpersonal skills as a coach.

Journal Prompt 15

What strengths do you bring to the coaching practice?

So You Think You Can Coach?

Journal Prompt 16

How do you build trust with your teachers? What have been some of your successes?

Journal Prompt 17

In what areas do you want to further develop your coaching skills?

Journal Prompt 18

How do you ensure that your feedback is constructive and specific?

Journal Prompt 19

How do you ensure your feedback is actionable?

So You Think You Can Coach?

Journal Prompt 20

How do you support teachers in reflecting on their practice?

Journal Prompt 21

Make a list of professional goals and topics that you feel you may need.

Journal Prompt 22

Reflect on your collaboration with stakeholders, such as administrators, parents, etc. How do you foster collaboration and build relationships with these individuals?

Journal Prompt 23

Write out some ways that you can measure and evaluate the effectiveness of your coaching interventions.

So You Think You Can Coach?

Journal Prompt 24

What strategies do you or can you use to advocate for the needs of teachers and students?

Journal Prompt 25

Reflect on your role as an advocate for effective instructional practices. How do you or can you promote a culture of continuous school improvement within your school or school district?

Journal Prompt 26

What is one thing that happened during your coaching today that you found to be positive?

Journal Prompt 27

What does the ideal day of coaching look like for you? Are there any things that you can implement to make sure that happens?

So You Think You Can Coach?

Journal Prompt 28

List three things that you are thankful for on this journey of coaching. Explain why you are thankful for those particular things.

Journal Prompt 29

Reflect on your work from the previous day. What could you have done more of and possibly better?

So You Think You Can Coach?

Journal Prompt 30

Sometimes we can't avoid the stress of the job or people that we are coaching. What is something that you will intentionally do to put stress in its proper place today?

Journal Prompt 31

We know that relationship building is vital for the coaching experience. What is one thing that you will do today to enhance a relationship for future coaching?

So You Think You Can Coach?

Journal Prompt 32

Think of a teacher that you feel you have not been able to quite connect with relationship-wise. Why do you think that is? Create a stepped-out plan for your next efforts to strengthen that relationship.

Journal Prompt 33

Think of a coach that you have been coached by. What were the aspects of that coach that you liked? What were the aspects of the coach that you did not like? We get to decide the type of coach that we will be.

So You Think You Can Coach?

Journal Prompt 34

Think of some teachers that you feel would benefit your coaching if you knew them a little better. Make a list of them. How would they add value to your coaching?

Journal Prompt 35

Reflect on some goals that you have set for the year. Write a congratulatory letter to yourself for meeting those goals.

Journal Prompt 36

Reflect on some goals that you have set for the year that have not yet come to fruition. How do you feel about this? What are some that you feel you still have time to accomplish? What is your plan of action to complete those?

Journal Prompt 37

What are some team goals that you have set that could use some refining? In what ways will you refine those goals?

So You Think You Can Coach?

Journal Prompt 38

Work plans are important for productivity. Write out or refine your work plan for the upcoming day and possibly the upcoming week.

Journal Prompt 39

In what ways can you become more productive as an instructional coach? Think of one thing you need to happen to increase your productivity. Discuss that request with your principal or district leaders.

So You Think You Can Coach?

Journal Prompt 40

Brainstorm a list of items that you feel your teachers would benefit modeling from. For each item, jot down who would be the best person to model that strategy for the teacher.

Journal Prompt 41

What are your strong suits that you feel would benefit teachers with your modeling?

So You Think You Can Coach?

Journal Prompt 42

Make a priority list of teachers who you feel need to be observed and given feedback. How will you address the list that you created? Consider placing days and times by their names.

Journal Prompt 43

Reflect on how PLCs are going. What are the strengths? What are the opportunities for growth?

So You Think You Can Coach?

Journal Prompt 44

What is motivating you right now? What will you try to implement in order to increase your own motivation as a coach?

Journal Prompt 45

How will you build or continue to build motivation with the teachers you are coaching? Put a short action plan in place.

So You Think You Can Coach?

Journal Prompt Prompt 46

Do you feel that those you are coaching trust you? Why or why not? What are some things you can do to cultivate that trust?

Journal Prompt Prompt 47

What is your personal definition of an effective instructional coach? Based on your personal definition, what are some areas that you can fine tune?

So You Think You Can Coach?

Journal Prompt Prompt 48

Based on your coaching, what is one thing that made you happy today or possibly yesterday? Why did it make you smile? Feel free to list more than one.

Journal Prompt 49

Why do you feel you are a good coach? You are definitely a good coach.

Journal Prompt 50

Reflect on any item or task that you can do that would make you feel more organized.

About The Author

Celeta Devine brings over two decades of experience in the field of education, coupled with a passion for empowering teachers and students alike. With a rich background spanning various roles within the educational landscape, Celeta has established himself/herself as a prominent figure in the realm of instructional coaching and leadership development.

Having served as a consultant and instructional coach for over nine years, Celeta has honed her expertise in supporting educators to enhance their instructional practices and maximize student learning outcomes. She has a proven track record of success, having been recognized as Teacher of the Year twice during her tenure in the classroom.

As a National Board Certified Teacher and the owner of Diverse Learning Practices Education, LLC, Celeta Devine is dedicated to promoting inclusive and effective teaching strategies that cater to the diverse needs of students. Through her consultation career, Celeta has had the privilege of coaching teachers in Mississippi and beyond, helping them unlock their full potential and achieve excellence in their profession.

In addition to her work in education, Celeta is the founder of L.E.A.D Leadership Excellence AND Direction, an initiative focused on developing leadership skills among teens and young adults. Her commitment to nurturing the next generation of leaders reflects her belief in the power of education to transform lives and communities.

Celeta holds a degree in English Education and a Specialist degree in Educational Leadership. Originally from the small town of Ellisville, MS, she has made significant contributions to the field of education both locally and nationally. She was featured in Bold Journey Magazine for her entrepreneurial endeavors, showcasing her dedication to innovation and continuous improvement in education.

Through her book "So You Think You Can Coach? 10 Instructional Plays That Build Teacher Capacity," Celeta shares her wealth of knowledge, practical insights, and transformative strategies for empowering educators to excel in their profession. She remains committed to championing excellence in education and making a positive impact on the lives of teachers and students alike.

Celeta Joyce Devine

Meet the Coaches

Coach Bobby Coleman:

Coach Bobby Coleman, a stalwart in the realm of coaching, brings to the field a rich tapestry of experience and wisdom honed over two decades. Graduating with a degree in Social Studies Education from Mississippi College, Coleman seamlessly blended his passion for education with his love for coaching. His journey is marked by previous titles such as Avid Educator and Passionate Coach, as well as Leadership Mentor and Character Development Coach, showcasing his multifaceted approach to shaping young minds and athletes. Coleman's dedication and prowess as a coach were recognized when he was named Former Instructor of the Year by MDOC, a testament to his profound impact beyond the sports arena.

In his illustrious coaching career spanning 20 years, Coleman has amassed a plethora of achievements and accolades, including being awarded the prestigious Head Coach of the Year for District 6 Class 4A in 2008. Additionally, his contributions to adult education were celebrated when he was named Adult Education Teacher of the Year, solidifying his status as a transformative figure in both academic and athletic spheres. Coleman's coaching philosophy is encapsulated in his poignant quote, "Failure occurs the moment you stop trying," a testament to his unwavering belief in the power of perseverance and resilience.

So You Think You Can Coach?

Coach Coleman's coaching style is characterized by his genuine demeanor and heart for people. He approaches coaching with pragmatism, leveraging his steady nature and level-headedness to guide his team to success. His commitment to nurturing not only the athletic abilities but also the character and personal growth of his players sets him apart as a coach of exceptional caliber.

Coach Dr. Chyenne Trussell:

Dr. Chyenne Trussell, a revered figure in the coaching realm, boasts an illustrious career spanning nearly four decades. With a robust educational background encompassing degrees from East Mississippi Community College, The University of Southern Mississippi, and Jackson State University, Dr. Trussell brings a wealth of knowledge and expertise to the field. His journey is punctuated by various titles, including Coach, Leadership Mentor, and Athletic Director of Schools, underscoring his multifaceted approach to coaching and mentorship.

Dr. Trussell's coaching journey is studded with notable achievements, including being recognized as the Clarion Ledger Coach of the Week and leading the Jackson Callaway football team to a commendable 8-3 season and playoffs berth in his first year as head coach. His tenure also saw numerous players receiving athletic scholarships to various colleges and universities, a testament to his prowess in developing talent and nurturing their potential.

Throughout his esteemed career, Dr. Trussell's coaching philosophy has been encapsulated in his profound quote, "Blossom where you are planted," emphasizing the importance of embracing one's circumstances and striving for excellence. His coaching style is characterized by his genuine love for people and his unwavering commitment to their growth and development. Dr. Trussell's ability to inspire and empower individuals to be their best selves transcends the realm of sports, making him a beloved figure in every environment he graces.

Coach Latisha Brown:

Coach Latisha Brown emerges as a trailblazer and inspirational figure in the world of coaching, boasting a remarkable career spanning over three decades. With degrees from the University of Phoenix and the University of Houston, including Organizational Management and Consumer Science, Brown's educational background lays a solid foundation for her coaching prowess. Her journey is marked by various titles, including Coach, Author, Inspirational Speaker, and Project Manager, reflecting her multifaceted approach to coaching and leadership.

Brown's coaching journey is punctuated by numerous achievements and milestones, including serving as the Captain of the United States

So You Think You Can Coach?

Olympic Festival North Team in 1991 and receiving the Club Coach of the Year award for her exemplary coaching at Willowbrook Sports Club. She also holds the distinction of being the first African-American to play club volleyball in the city of Houston and the first in her family to become a Division I coach, coaching at prestigious institutions such as the University of Houston and Rice University.

Coach Brown's coaching philosophy is encapsulated in her mantra, "The DAS Effect," which emphasizes the fusion of Discipline, Action, and Success. Her coaching style is characterized by a holistic approach that encompasses the physical, emotional, and spiritual well-being of her athletes. Brown's depth of experience and commitment to nurturing the potential of those she comes in contact with make her a phenomenal coach and mentor, leaving an indelible impact on all those she encounters.

Coach Tony Vance:

Coach Tony Vance stands as a paragon of leadership and excellence in the realm of coaching, boasting an impressive career spanning over 27 years. With degrees from Coahoma Community College and Mississippi Valley State University, including a Masters from Mississippi Valley State University, Vance's educational journey laid a solid foundation for his coaching prowess. His journey is marked by various titles, including Coach and Principal Athletic

Celeta Joyce Devine

Director of Schools, highlighting his multifaceted approach to coaching and leadership.

Vance's coaching journey is punctuated by numerous achievements and accolades, including multiple Coach of the Year awards and leading Charleston High School to a State Championship in 2011. He also served as the President of the Mississippi Association of Coaches and had the honor of coaching the Mississippi/Alabama All-Star Game, further cementing his status as a transformative figure in the coaching realm.

Throughout his esteemed career, Coach Vance's coaching philosophy has been encapsulated in his profound quote, "Culture drives expectations and beliefs; expectations and beliefs drive behavior; behavior drives habits, and habits create your future," emphasizing the importance of fostering a positive and empowering environment. His coaching style is characterized by his ability to ignite fire and passion in his players and coaches, coupled with his down-to-earth demeanor and effective communication skills. Vance's unwavering commitment to excellence and positive change make him a cherished figure in the coaching community, leaving a lasting legacy of success on and off the field.